The *prima materia* of Myanmar Buddhist culture

Laukathara of Rakhine Thu Mrat

Translated and explained by
Shwe Lu Maung

မြန်မာဗုဒ္ဓ ယဉ်ကျေးမှု အနှစ်သာရ
ရခိုင်သူမြတ် ၏ လောကသာရ

ရွှေလူမောင်
ဘာသာပြန် ရှင်းလင်းသည်

A publication of
Shahnawaz Khan
USA

ISBN 10: 1-928840-15-9

ISBN 13: 978-1-928840-15-2

Library of Congress Control Number: 2015956223

Cover photo: An Oap (အုပ်), Myanmar traditional lacquered ceremonial bowl, on the Pann (ပန်း) lacquered tray.

The covers and the interior are designed and edited by the Khan Publication team. Paperback proof date November 28, 2015.

Printed and Published in USA by Shahnawaz Khan.

Website: http://www.shwelumaung.org

MADE IN USA

To my parents

To my parents

Table of Contents

Extended contents

Laukathara extended contents

Appendices extended contents

Acknowledgment

I live with an infinite debt of gratitude to my parents, U Maung Tha Pru and Daw San Win, who taught me *Laukathara* since I was a child. Also, I am indebted to my teacher U Nga Aung who taught me history and literature in my school days. As the time goes by, their teachings give me deep and clear insight into *Laukathara* and its implications in Myanmar culture and politics. On the strength of their teachings, I am confident in translating and interpreting *Laukathara* for the international audience.

Equally, I am grateful to my siblings, friends, and colleagues who have given me full support during the process of the translation. Especially, my thanks are due to my colleagues from the Department of Burmese at Magwe College (now Magway University) for sharing their knowledge of *Laukathara* and its important place in Myanmar cultural literature.

Finally, I would like to record my thanks to my family and the Khan Publication Team for reviewing and helping me improved the style and design of the translation and the book.

SLM
October 14, 2015

Introduction

Objectives of the translation

There are two objectives in my endeavor of translating *Lauka-thara (The Essence of the World)* into English.

The first objective is:

To present the international community with a piece of Myanmar classic cultural philosophy which has a significant political bearing.

The second objective is:

To give a glimpse of a Myanmar classic literature to the world and especially to the Myanmar diaspora who may not have the opportunity of learning Myanmar language and literature.

Culture and literature

Laukathara teaches how to be a Buddhist, how to build a Buddhist society, and how to be a Buddhist king. In its poetic verses, *Laukathara* illustrates the fabrics of Myanmar Buddhist culture with bright and colorful words. From learning *Laukathara*, one can also gain mastery of Myanmar literature. *Laukathara* or 'The Essence of the World' is based on the Theravada Buddhism. Hence, the Theravada Buddhism or 'Elder's Doctrine' is the *prima materia* of the teaching. Therefore, a student of *Laukathara* will also be rewarded with proficiency in Buddhist teaching and in the way it is practiced day-to-day.

I grew up with *Laukathara* and *Puttowada*, the two most famous Myanmar literature written in a genre of poems known as "pyo" (ပျို့).   The two "pyo" represent the core of Myanmar culture. My parents were well versed in the literature and they recited the famous verses and stanza easily and freely, in their free time.   They taught me the meanings and goodness of the verses, which are filled with credible advice. I also learned many verses of these "pyo" at school. Among the two "pyo", *Laukathara* is most comprehensive since it is written for all ages of people, the royals,   and the intellectuals (Ponna) whereas

Puttowada, which means "the advice to a son," entirely puts the focus on a growing son. *Laukathara* represents ethics, culture, philosophy, and fabrics of the Myanmar Buddhist society. Written in or around 1333 CE, *Laukathara* also holds the credit of the first "pyo" ever written in Myanmar, hence the origin of Myanmar literature.

A "pyo" is the simplest form of a poem in Myanmar literature. In particular, a book written in simple poems is called a "pyo." Each stanza of a pyo generally consists of four words, making four syllables. Each Myanmar word has only one syllable. For example, when written in English "Myanmar" is one word with two syllables. However, when written in Myanmar language it is Myan (မြန်) + Mar (မာ) and constitutes two words and two syllables, because "Myan" and "Mar" also have their own meanings. Thus, literally, Myanmar means "quick recovery" from an illness. Nonetheless, Myanmar is a name believed to have derived from Brahma, the heavenly beings of Buddhist cosmology, who created the universe.

The rules of rhyming in a Pyo are very flexible. In general, it rhymes 4,3,2 as shown in Table-1. However, it can also rhyme 4,2, 4,1, and 4,3,1, as shown in Table-2 and Table-3 respectively.

Table-1. Classic 4,3,2 rhyming in a "p-yo" Example from verse 3, stanza 1 to 3, page 3			
1	2	3	4
သူ	ကြီး	မိ	ဘ
thu	gyi	mi	ba
ဆ	ယ	သ	သား
hsa	ya	sa	thah
စိုး	ရ	သ	ခင်
soe	ya	tha	khin

Table-2. Flexible 4,2; 4,1 rhyming in a "p-yo"
Example from verse 2, stanza 1 to 3, page 1

1	2	3	4
အ	သက်	ရည်	စွာ
ah	thek	yheh	swah
အ	နာ	မဲ့	ကြောင်း
ah	nah	mae	Kyaung
ကောင်း	လှ	စေ	ချင်
kaung	hla	sae	chin

Table-3. Flexible 4,3,1 rhyming in a "p-yo"
Example from verse 20, stanza 16-18, page 16

1	2	3	4
နေ့	နား	ပျော်	ရှိုင်
nay	nah	pyau	shewin
ထို	သစ်	ပင်	ကား
Hto	thit	pin	gah
ဝင်	လာ	သ	သူ
Win	la	tha	thu

The shadings indicate the rhymes. In the tables, the English transliteration is based on the Bama pronunciation because Bama version serves as the national language. However, Rakhine Thu Mrat wrote *Laukathara* with the Rakhine phonetics and it reads best with the Rakhine pronunciation.

Author and history

Laukatraha is believed to have written in or around 1333 CE by a Rakhine Buddhist Bikkhu, known as Rakhine Thu Mrat or Rakhine Holy Man, to teach his students. It was a summary of his teachings. He was the teacher of King Mun Hti (r.1279-1385 CE, Laung Krut Dynasty). King Min Hti entrusted him with the education of three Burmese (Thet or Chakma) princes, namely Saw Son, Saw Pru, and Saw Tu. They were the sons of King Lyin Saw who was the king of the Chakma (*Thet*). His kingdom Thayet or Thet Yet, meaning the Chakma Province, was seized in 1333 CE by the Rakhine King Mun Hti as the Chakma people marauded the Rakhine border villages. Today, the City of Thayet is at the border of central and lower Myanmar. King Lyin Saw and his family were taken to Rakhine while the Rakhine Minister Razasithu Thungran was made the Governor of Thayet. Rakhine King Mun Hti was famous for his honesty and promise-keeping. He looked after King Lyin Saw and his family well, thus giving a good opportunity for the young Myanmar princes to pursue education. Even though the historians refer to them as the Myanmar or Thet princes their first name *Saw,* which is the last name of their father, indicates the Pyu lineage. Some names of earlier generations of Pagan kings in the pre-Anawrahta era are Pyu Saw Hti, Hti Min Yin, Yin Min Pike, Pike Thay Lay, Thay Lay Kyuw, and Kyuw Du Rit. The father's last name becomes the child's first name. Similarly, King Lyin Saw had three sons bearing the names, Saw Son, Saw Pru, and Saw Tu. Of the three brothers, Saw Tu later became King of Ava with the title of Sao Swa Ke. It is interesting to note that '*Sao*' is a Shan title and '*Saw*' is a Karen title, as well.

In the days of Rakkhapura dynasties the Buddhist monasteries were the universities, designed after the ancient Taxila (Takshashila), which was the biggest university established by Emperor Asoka (b.304?, r. 269-232 BCE) in western India, now Pakistan. Traditionally, sixteen subjects including the science of war and Buddhism were taught to the children of nobles and kings, regardless of sex. Rakhine Thu Mrat was the head monk, or Professor and President, of such a university. When the three princes grew up they became dukes (Myo Hsar) of Myin Sai Myo, Pyi Myo, and Amyint Myo respectively. Later, Amyint Myo Hsar Saw Tu (Taraphya Saw Ke) was elected by the ministers and nobles to the throne of Ava adopting the title, King Sao Swa Ke (r.1367-1404 CE), at the death of the founding King Thadoe Minphya (r.1364-1367 CE). He was elected on the merit that he was a descendant of Pagan Dynasty (1044-1291 CE) and Shan Dynasty (1298-1364 CE). The interlude between the end of Pagan Dynasty and the beginning of Shan dynasty is due to the Mongol Chinese Emperor Kublai Khan's occupation of Myanmar in 1279 CE.

On the 16th year of his reign, King Sao Swa Ke invited his aging teacher Rakhine Thu Mrat to his kingdom. He worshiped and honored him with the title of *Maha Thingha Raza,* which means *Great Lord Sanga.* Thus, *Laukathara* reached Myanmar from Rakkhapura and became a royal handbook of the Myanmar Kings as well. It is then that the Rakhine and the Myanmar merged into a common written heritage of cultural norms, and royal administrative philosophy. It was a source of unity between the two historically hostile peoples, the Rakhine and the Bama.

Culture and Politics

Laukathara has been in use as a guiding source of law and order, rules and regulations, ethics and philosophy, and traditions and cultures in the society as well as in the royal administration of Myanmar since the days of Rakhine King Mun Hti (r.1279-1385 CE, Laung Krut Dynasty) and King Sao Swa Ke (r.1367-1404 CE) of Ava. Thus, it has been the heart of Myanmar culture nearly 700 years.

It has three parts. Part 1, *Advice to the four kinds of people,* teaches ethics to the people at large and shows the ways how to live a good life. Part 2 is addressed to the king and the royals, and is comparable to *The Prince* of Niccolo Machiavelli (1498-1527 CE), in view of the government mechanism. The *Advice to the Ponna* or the intellectuals, in Part 3, elucidates the influence of Vedic culture on Myanmar society. In addition, *Laukathara* advises the people and the intellectuals to be loyal to the king. Fundamentally, *Laukathara* lays down a Buddhist doctrine which serves as not only the foundation but also the fabrics of a society and kingdom. Hence, *Laukathara* constitutes the *prima materia* of Myanmar Buddhist culture.

In the modern days, it came to its political prominence when Senior General Saw Maung announced that he would rule the country according to *Laukathara* in 1990. His adoption of *Laukathara* as the ruling doctrine officially ushered Buddhist norms into Myanmar politics. In the recent days, since 2007, the world is seeing the rise of "Buddhist nationalism" with the symptoms of racial and religious intolerance and violence in Myanmar. The reader will be familiar with the news of the rising nationalist Buddhist organization known as *ma-ba-tha*, which is the acronym of the *a-myo batha tharthanah saunt shaught yey a-faweat* (အမျိုးဘာသာ သာသနာ စောင့်ရှောက်ရေးအဖွဲ့). So far, *mabatha* has been successful in its mass movement to introduce four *Race and Religion Protection Laws* in the Myanmar Parliament, which adopted them with large majority. Myanmar President Thein Sein signed the laws into effect in September 2015. In the media reports, *mabatha* is translated into English in various forms such as Association for the Protection of Race and Religion, Organization for the Protection of Race and Religion and Committee for the Protection of Nationality and Religion. However, the meaningful translation should be *Organization for the Protection of Race, Culture and Religion,* see Table-4.

Table-4	
a-myo batha tharthanah saunt shaught yey a-faweat	
(အမျိုးဘာသာ သာသနာ စောင့်ရှောက်ရေးအဖွဲ့)	
Organization for the Protection of Race, Culture and Religion	
Myanmar	English Translation
a-myo	race
*batha**	Culture
tharthanah	religion
saunt shaught	protection
yey	for
a-faweat	organization
* *batha-sagah* is language	

The philosophy and objectives of *mabatha* are the same as those of the Young Men's Buddhist Association (YMBA), which initiated the independence movement in the British Burma. Therefore, it is not a new phenomenon. As a matter of fact, the *prima materia* that gives the *mabatha*'s philosophy and objectives can be found in *Laukathara*. That is why, understanding of *Laukathara* also means the understanding of Myanmar culture and society, including her political fabrics.

The structure

Laukathara is composed of three parts, Part-1 *Advice to the four kinds of people*, Part-2 *Advice to the king*, and Part-3 *Advice to the Ponna*. Overall, it is constructed with a total of 55 verses, 1642 stanzas, and 5495 words. The breakdown of the stanza and word counts is given in Table-5.

The Source

The Myanmar version used in this translation is from *Rakhine Thu Mrat Laukathara-pyo*, presented and explained by Min Thuu Wun, and published by Lin Oo Tara Hsapey, Yangon, 1996 when the State Law and Order Restoration Council was in power. Min Thuu Wun (1909-2004) is a *guru*, meaning he is more than a professor of Burmese literature. He was a pioneer of modern Myanmar literature renaissance, decorated with the national honors of *Wunna Kyaw Htin* and *Thiri Pyanchi*. Min Thuu Wun was a pro-military person and the military junta used him as a Cultural Attaché in the foreign services. On the 16th of March 2016, Min Thuu Wun's son, Htin Kyaw, became the first civilian president of Myanmar in 54 years since the military *coup d'état* on 2nd March, 1962.

Originally, *Laukathara* was written on the palm leaves. Due to the long period of reproduction in palm-leaf writing there exists variant forms of stanzas. Min Thuu Wun listed a total of 166 variant stanzas, approximately 10% of the total 1642 stanzas. Only the three verses, i.e., verse 1, verse 2, and verse 5 are free of the variant version of stanza (Table-5). However, the variant forms do not change the meaning of the verses. The variant forms simply represent a choice of alternative words and rhyming, but still convey similar meanings in the core. Min Thuu Wun's book is not free of press errors, but the errors are minor and can easily be corrected. I have stayed within the limit of Min Thuu Wun's version. However, in few cases, Table-6, I have used the stanzas that reflect more of the Rakhine tradition.

Table-5. The Structure of *Laukathara*

	Verse	1	2	3	4	5	6	7	8	9	10	11	12	13
P A R T 1	Stanza count	13	14	13	14	14	14	15	14	14	16	14	23	21
	Word count	48	59	55	59	61	59	63	59	59	69	59	95	87
	Variant stanza			1	2		1	4	2	3	2	1	3	3
	Verse	**14**	**15**	**16**	**17**	**18**	**19**	**20**	**21**	**22**				
	Stanza count	18	24	23	23	20	29	32	23	9				
	Word count	75	99	95	96	83	124	131	95	39				
	Variant stanza	1	4	4	1	1	9	7	3	1				
P A R T 2	**Verse**	**23**	**24**	**25**	**26**	**27**	**28**	**29**	**30**	**31**	**32**	**33**	**34**	**35**
	Stanza count	28	23	22	23	22	22	25	27	42	40	43	37	44
	Word count	116	95	91	96	91	91	103	111	171	163	175	152	179
	Variant stanza	3	3	1	6	4	4	3	5	2	4	6	7	7
	Verse	**36**	**37**	**38**	**39**	**40**	**41**	**42**	**43**	**44**	**45**	**46**	**47**	
	Stanza count	41	39	50	40	51	56	42	57	45	52	49	25	
	Word count	169	120	203	165	207	228	171	231	183	212	199	104	
	Variant stanza	1	6	5	6	7	3	5	8	8	4	2	3	
P A R T 3	**Verse**	**48**	**49**	**50**	**51**	**52**	**53**	**54**	**55**					
	Stanza count	46	39	41	46	39	37	33	16					
	Word count	189	161	167	187	159	152	138	69					
	Variant stanza	7	6	3	6	4	2	3	2					

Table-6. The variant stanzas I have used		
Verse and Stanza	Variant stanza I use	Min Thuu Wun's version
v15, s24	အိုသော် လူမရယ်စေနှင့်မင်း	အိုသော် သူမရယ်စေနှင့်မင်း
v19, s24	စီးပွားလာဟု	စီးပွားလာအံ့
v20, s1 and 2	ကျောင်းတော်ခရီး၊ လမ်းမကြီး၌	ကြောင်းပါးခရီး၊ လမ်းအနီး၌
v32, s25	အူချာမွန်မှု	ဦးဖျားမွန်မှု
v34, s25	ရတနာမြဂူ	ရတနာမြတ်ဂူ
v37, s8	အလွန်ဖျင်ပြဲ	ပြည့်လွန်ဖျင်ပြဲ
v39, s10	လည်ပင်းခြေရှည်	လည်ပင်းခပ်ရှည်
v40, s47	နှင်ခြောက်ခြိမ်းမောင်း	နှင်ချောက်ခြိမ်းမောင်း
v45, s21	မခဲစိမ့်ငှာ	ရှောင်ဖဲစိမ့်ငှာ၊
v48, s10	ဟူးရားကြယ်မြင်	ဟူးရားကျမ်းမြင်
v48, s39	သလိပ်များက	သလိပ်ဖျားက
v54, s25	နည်းနာသိပွ	နာနာသိပွ

Translation

If the Myanmar version **လောကသာရ** (Laukathara) were written in Pali Devanagari script it will be लोक सार (loka-sāra). In English, *loka* is the world and *sāra* is the essence.

In general, I go for an adaptive translation. However, this translation also goes stanza by stanza, in order to get closest to the original meaning. The explanations of many Pali or Sanskrit words are given in the footnotes, and for complicated words in the appendices. Overall, I am confident that the translation will give a good overview with a sharp focus on the subject of interest.

Shwe Lu Maung
March 21, 2016

လောကသာရ
ရခိုင်သူမြတ်

ပထမပိုင်း
အမျိုးလေးပါးဆုံးမခန်း

Laukathara
Rakhine Thu Mrat

Part 1
Advice to the four kinds of people

Translated and explained by Shwe Lu Maung

၁။

ကြားပိမ့်သူမြတ်၊ အများမှတ်စိမ့်။ ဟိတတ္တိက၊ သြဝါဒဖြင့်၊
ဆုံးမပေးထွေ၊ နားဝင်စေလော့။ နေသို့ထင်ရှား၊
ဘုရား တရား သံဃာ၊ ရတနာထွတ်ထား၊ မြတ်သုံးပါးကို၊
ဦးဖျားထိပ်ထက်၊ အမြဲရွက်ရှို့၊ စုံမက်သဒ္ဓါ ကြည်စေမင်း။   ။

1.

I, Thu Mrat, shall speak; so, people may learn.
This is a beneficial teaching.
Give ear with due attention.
Brilliant as the sun are the Buddha,
The Dhamma, and the Sangha.
Always wear the Three Jewels
On the top of the forehead,
And cherish them with love and devotion.

၂။

အသက်ရှည်စွာ၊ အနာမဲ့ကြောင်း၊ ကောင်းလှစေချင်၊
ပွဲပြင်နိစ္စ၊ ကွပ်ဆုံးမသား၊ မိဘဆရာ၊ စကားနာရှို့၊
ကျမ်းစာသိမြင်၊ တတ်အောင်သင်လော့။
ပေါ်လွင်မပြု၊ ကောင်းရာတုလျက်၊ ကောင်းမှုမြတ်နိုး၊
ကောင်းအောင်ကြိုးရှို့၊ ကောင်းကျိုး ကိုယ်၌ တည်စေမင်း။   ။

2.

For a long life, free of illness,
Wishing you best,
Giving guidance, discipline and advice,
Are the parents and the teachers.
Pay ears to their words;
Study the books,
See the wisdom, and learn the knowledge.
Avoid the vanities,
Culture good manners,
Love to be good,
Strive to be good, and
Institute in you good.

၃॥
သူကြီးမိဘ၊ ဆရာစသား၊ စိုးရသခင်၊ ကျေးဇူးရှင်တို့၊
ပြစ်တင်မောင်းမဲ့၊ ရိုက်ပုတ်ဆဲလည်း၊ ဝမ်းထဲယုံ့ယုံ့၊
ယုန်လျှင်ကျူ့သို့၊ ဆိုတို့မဝှဲ့၊ စောင်မာန်ညှို့ရှို့၊
ကြောက်ရွံ့ရှိသေ၊ သည်းခံထွေဖြင့်၊
ကောင်းတေ နှလုံး ရှည်စေမင်း॥

3.
The elders, the parents, and the teachers,
Also the governing authorities;
They are the Benefactors.
The Benefactors may
    criticize, scold, and even punish you.
But, you must
    take these with a soft stomach,
Like a rabbit humbles itself.
Do not rebut; do not argue;
Keep your temper soft and controlled;
Show your respect and fear;
Be tolerant.
Thus,
    Let the good heart of yours be infinite.

၄॥
ဆန္ဒဒေါသာ၊ ဘယာမောဟ၊ အပါယ်ကျသား၊ ဓမ္မလေးမည်၊
ဂတိတည်ရှို့၊ လူ့ပြည်နတ်ရွာ၊ ချမ်းသာကောင်းမွန်၊ စံစုန်ဆန်လျက်၊
နိဗ္ဗာန် ရောက်ကြောင်း၊ ကျင့်ကောင်းသီလ၊ လျှူဒါနနှင့်၊
ပုညလယ်မြေ၊ စိုက်ကြိုထွေဖြင့်၊ ပျိုးခြေအပင် စည်စေမင်း॥ ॥

4.
The desire, the anger, the fear, and the delusion;
These are the four sins that lead to hell.
Be mindful of the Four Dhamma;[1]

---
[1] The Four Dhamma (ဓမ္မလေးမည်), see the Appendix-1, p 104

Let you be born and reborn
 in the peaceful, serene and
 good places of Human World
 and Heaven Villages.
Nurture the path to Nibban;[2]
Practice good moral; Give charities;
Seed and plant the crops of good merits.
This is the way to enrich the good virtues.

၅။

ကိုယ်နှုတ်နှလုံး၊ စောင့်သုံးမြဲစွာ၊ သတ္တဝါကို၊ မေတ္တာသက်ပေ၊
လှူဖို့ဝေ၍၊ စိတ်စေကြည်သန့်၊ သဘောမှန်သား၊
ပစ္စုပ္ပန် သံသရာ၊ ချမ်းသာစီးပွား၊ နှစ်ပါးမြင်တတ်၊
သူတော်မြတ်ကို၊ မပြတ်ချစ်ခင်၊ မိတ်ကျွမ်းဝင်၍၊
မြဲပင် စင်းလျင်း ပေါင်းယှဉ်မင်း။ ။

5.

Be watchful of the body, the tongue, and the heart.
Be loving to all living things.
Share your merits with all.
Let your mind be strong with serenity.
Cherish the right moral.
A Holy Person is the one who can see
 peace and prosperity at the present
 and in the Samsara.[3]
To such a Holy Person,
 always render friendship with love.
Let the friendship be strong
 and long-lasting.

---

[2] Nirvana, Enlightenment
[3] Samsara, cycles of birth and rebirths in Buddhism

၅။

ပညာမျက်စိၣ မြင်မရှိ၍၊ မသိတရား၊ အယူမှားလျက်၊ စီးပွားမမြော်၊
ကျိုးမပေါ်သား၊ သူတော်မဟုတ်၊ ယုတ်သည်စရိုက်၊ လူသူမိုက်ကို၊
မကြိုက်မချစ်၊ ရန်သူစစ်သို့၊ မနှစ်သက်ပဲ၊ ဝေးစွာရဲ၍၊
အမြဲစွာရှင်း ဖဲကြဉ်မင်း။။ ။

6.

The eyes of knowledge, when lack,
The truth is not known;
The wrong prevails;
Prosperity is blocked;
Goodness is absent.
Such are the characters of
   a foolish human.
To such a foolish human,
Do not endow love or liking.
Consider the foolish human
   a true enemy;
Disapproved and stay way,
Always keep a distance
   and avoid from afar.

၇။

ပါဏာတိပါတ်၊ မသတ်သူ့သက်၊ ခိုးဒွက်မမှု၊ မယူသေစာ၊
အိမ်ရာမမှား၊ မုသားမဆို၊ ကိုယ်ကိုနှိမ့်ချ၊ စောင့်သီလနှင့်၊
ဒါနလှူဝတ်၊ ရက်မချွတ်လျှင်၊ မပြတ်ဆောက်တည်၊
ဆုကြီးရည်၍၊ မကြည်ခိုက်ရန်၊ သူကျူးလွန်လည်း၊
မျက်မာန်မပြင်း သိမ်းလေမင်း။။ ။

7.

No killing,
No stealing,
No drinking,
No adultery,
No telling lies.

Be humble and
maintain the Sila;[4]
Give charity every day;
Always strive with
    the goal of Great Trophy.[5]
Even if someone commits animosity and quarrel,
Control the anger and respond with restraint.

၇ ॥

မိခင်ဖခင်၊[6] ကျေးဇူးရှင်ကို၊ ချစ်ခင်မြတ်နိုး၊ ဂူပုထိုးသို့၊
ရှိခိုးဦးတင်၊ ကြည်လင်မြတ်လေး၊ သိမ်းမြန်း မွေးရှို၊
လုပ်ကျွေးခယ၊ ရှိတုပ်ကွလျက်၊ ကြီးထသက်အို၊
မျိုးဆွေကိုလည်း၊ ကြည်ညိုညွတ်တိမ်း၊ ပိုက်ထုပ်သိမ်းရှို၊
မယဲမ်းစင်းလျင်း ငြိမ်းစေမင်း॥   ॥

8.

The mother and the father
    are the Benefactors.
Love them fondly;
Respect them in the same way
    you respect a pagoda.
With reverence and adoration,
In their advanced age,
    keep them in your fold.
Look after them with humility
    and respect.

---

[4] Sila, precepts; the good moral practices. No killing/stealing/drinking/adultery/telling lies are the basic Five Sila that one must keep at all time.

[5] Great Trophy means Nibban (Nirvana) in this context.

[6] As per traditions, Buddha said the mother must be placed above the father because she carries the child in her womb and feeds the baby her breast. Buddha showed Dhamma to his mother in heaven and his mother attained Arahatship, Nibbana, and Enlightenment. The Path to Enlightenment *is the greatest thing* one can give in the universe. Even then, Buddha said his providence of the Path to Enlightenment does not compensate even a drop of the mother's milk he suckled. In light of this teaching and story, the Myanmar Buddhists say "mother and father" but not "father and mother."

Similarly, do the same for the aged
    and the relatives.
With respect and humbleness,
    provide your care.
With a straight heart,
    Let there be peace of mind.

၉။

စတုဒိသာ၊ လေးမျက်နှာမှ၊ ရောက်လှာအများ၊ ပုဏ္ဏား ရဟန်း၊
ဆွမ်းပန်းချို့တဲ့၊ ရိက္ခာမဲ့ကို၊ ဆည်းခဲ့ဥစ္စာ၊ အိမ်လှောင်ခါ၌၊
လွယ်ကာထားယူ၊ ထိုသသူကို၊ ကိုယ်တူမှတ်သား၊ သနားမြတ်လေး၊
ဝတ်စားပေး၍၊ ကျွေးမွေးထံရင်း ငြိမ်းစေမင်း။ ။

9.

From the four horizons,
From the four corners,
There come Ponna[7] and Monks.
They are the people of austerity;
They lack food and supplies.
Save and maintain some food
    and supplies for such persons.
Take them as if they were you in yourself;
Be kind and show respect to them;
Provide food and clothing to them;
Under your care, let them find peace.

၁၀။

အနိစ္စနှင့်၊ ဒုက္ခအနတ္တား၊ သုံးပါးလက္ခဏာ၊
မချာအောက်မေ့၊ တစ္ဆေစ္ဆေလျှင်၊ အလေ့အလာ၊
ကွပ်ဆုံးမ၍၊ ပဥ္စခန္ဓာ၊ ငါးဖြာနာမ်ရုပ်၊ ဖြစ်ချုပ်ကြိမ်ဖန်၊
စက်အဟန်သို့၊ ဖန်တလဲလဲ၊ ဝဋ်ဆင်းရဲကို၊ ဝမ်းထဲသံဝေ၊
ထိတ်လန့်တွေဖြင့်၊ ရှီးရေသည်းတွင်း ကြိမ်းစေမင်း။ ။

---

[7] Ponna is a Vedic priest or astrologer.

Translated and explained by Shwe Lu Maung

10.

Anicca, Dukkha, Anatta;[8]
Are the Three Doctrines.
Let these be
    in your mind without negligence,
Apply them and develop a discipline.
The Five Aggregates[9] of Mind and Body,
Originate and end in numerous cycles,
Like a movement of machine;
Repeated cyclic birth and rebirth is the suffering of Waht.[10]
Beware of it with repent and fear in your stomach;
Inside your bones and within your heart,
Live with conscience.

၁၁॥

လောဘ ဒေါသ၊ မောဟသူပျက်၊ နေ့တိုင်းဖျက်ရှ၍၊
အမျက်သည်းလွန်၊ တဖျင်သန်လျှက်၊ ပြေးလွန်ဖင်ဖင်၊
အာရုံမြင်က၊ ခင်ခင်မွတ်မွတ်၊ လိုက်လံတတ်သား၊
ထူးပွတ်မဆိုင်း၊ စိတ်ဆင်ရိုင်းကို၊ ထုံးပိုင်းမချာ၊
ယဉ်စိမ့်ငှါလျှင်၊ ပညာထိန်း၍ မိန်းစေမင်း॥   ॥

11.

Greed, anger, and delusion;
These are the evils
    that destroy you every day.
Furious and malevolent,
Everywhere and every time,
With passion, chasing the desires;
Extreme and uncontrolled is the 'mind',
    the 'Wild Elephant'.
For sure, beyond doubt,

---

[8] Anicca (Impermanency), Dukkha (Suffering), Anatta (nonexistence of self or soul) are the three main doctrines of the Buddha's teachings. See Appendix-2, p 105

[9] Five Aggregates ပၪၥခန္ဓာ, see the Appendix-3, p 106

[10] 'Waht' (Pali: vadham, vadha) is a punishment of Karma (inflicted by one's own action), that no one, even Buddha, can avoid.

You must tame it;
With your wisdom,
Keep it calm.

၁၂။

လယ်လုပ်ကုန်သွယ်၊ ကြွေးဆယ်မြီချ၊ တွက်ဆစိပ်ပြား၊
အပါးပါးလျှင်၊ အပွားအရင်း၊ လတွင်းတက်တိုး၊
ထမ်းပိုးနှစ်လည်၊ ချသည်မပြတ်၊ အိမ်ထောင်ဝတ်ဖြင့်၊
အမှတ်မြဲမြဲ၊ လုပ်ကြိုးကြိုးစား၊ ကျွဲနွားဆိတ်ဝက်၊
ဝမ်းဘဲ့ခွက်နှင့်၊ ကြက်ကမကြွင်း၊ သိမ်းမွေးပြင်းလျှက်၊
များခြင်းစုံစီ၊ ဖန်တီဝယ်ရောင်း၊ ထပ်ကာလောင်းလျှက်၊
ပဲပြောင်းစပါး၊ ကျီပြည့်ထားရှု၊ ခွက်ပြားရွှေငွေ၊
ဆည်းပူးတွေဖြင့်၊ မျိုးဆွေမှီတင်း ကြွယ်စေမင်း။ ။

12.

Farming and trading; loan and lending;
In all diversities of business and financing;
Capital and profit; Prosperity within a month;
With due diligence, perform the annual harvest and trade;
Such is the way of family duty.
With this in mind, work hard and plan well.
Buffaloes, cattle, goats, pigs, ducks, fowls, including the
chickens;
Husband all well; buy and sell all well.
Stock the legumes, corns, and
        paddy barnful.
Buy and save gold and silver,
In forms of cups and coins.
In this way, let you be wealthy
        and be a shelter of friends and relatives.

၁၃။
ထုံးတီးနည်းနာ၊ အဖြာဖြာ၍၊ ပညာရှာမီး၊ မကြီးသက်ရွယ်၊
အငယ်သော်က၊ ကြိုးလုံ့လလျက်၊ တုပ်ကွပုဆစ်၊ ဆရာစစ်၍၊
ကြောက်ချစ်ရိုသေ၊ လုပ်ကျွေးထွေဖြင့်၊ စာပေတတ်ကြောင်း၊
တချောင်းချောင်းလျှင်၊ ခြိမ်းမောင်းသည်းခံ၊ ဆရာထံ၍၊
သင်အံကျက်လေ့၊ တစ်နေ့တစ်ပါး၊ မှတ်သားလေလေ၊ ဝမ်းထဲ့ခွေ၍၊
အထွေအထူး၊ ဂုဏ်ကျေးဇူးကို၊ ဆည်းပူးသန့်ရှင်း ကြွယ်စေမင်း။ ။

13.
The arts, the science, and the technology;
There are many disciplines of knowledge.
Learn with great effort when you are young,
    before you grow old.
Find a good teacher. Be an obedient student.
Love, respect, and serve him well.
Set your mind for learning,
Strive and work hard with persistence.
With tolerance, take all harsh words
    and hard assignments.
Under the care of the teacher,
Learn, read, and recite day in and day out;
Remember and store all your learning,
    spiraling in your stomach.
Cherish and honor the teacher, the Beneficent.
As such, let yourself be rich and enriched.

၁၄။
ဘေးဘိုးစဉ်ဆက်၊ မပျက်သုံးစွဲ၊ ကျင့်မြဲလေ့လ၊ စာရိတ္တဖြင့်၊
မိဘအလိုက်၊ စရိုက်ကျင့်ရိုး၊ အမျိုးနွယ်လျဉ်၊ စောင့်စည်းကြဉ်၍၊
အယှဉ်အပေါင်း၊ ခင်ပွန်းကောင်းနှင့်၊ သူဟောင်းသက်ကြီး၊
ထုံးနည်းတီးကို၊ မငြီးမငွေ့၊ မှတ်ကျက်လေ့လျက်၊ ချောသွေ့စကား၊
စပ်ကြားသူပျက်၊ ကုန်းတိုက်ဖျက်လည်း၊ ရက်ရက်မယုံလေနှင့်မင်း။ ။

14.

Generations after generations,
Practices without failures,
Established traditions, with good characters.
The path of the parents,
Customs and codes of conduct,
In accord with the caste,
One must follow and conserve.
Keep friendship with good people.
From aged and old people,
Learn their knowledge and techniques,
Without feeling bored or tired.
There will be words of discord
    created by the outsiders.
Even when such subversion is in action,
Don't let yourself be fooled.

၁၅။

သူတော်တကာ၊ တတ်စရာသား၊ အဋ္ဌာရသ၊ သိပ္ပအပြား၊
အတတ်များကို၊ မှတ်သားသတိ၊ ပညာရှိတို့၊ တတ်သိအပ်စွ။
ထိုသိပ္ပကို၊ နှံ့မျှလုံးခြို၊ မတတ်တုံလည်း၊ တစ်စုံတစ်ခု၊
တတ်အောင်ပြု၍၊ လူမှုအိမ်ထောင်၊ စီးပွားဆောင်လော။
ညဉ့်မှောင်မသိ၊ ကြက်မျက်စိသို့၊ မိမိကိုယ်ဖို့၊ အတတ်ချို့သော်၊
သူတို့ပြစ်တင်၊ ဆင်းရဲဖျင်အံ့။
ထင်ထင်မျက်မြော်၊ မကော်ရော်သည်၊ အိုသော် လူမရယ်စေနှင့်မင်း။ ။

15.

Everyone has to learn;
There exist arts and science
and vast knowledge,
That a person may learn to become learned.
It may be hard to master
    every branch of arts and science.
Nevertheless,
    master a discipline of knowledge
So that you may bring wealth

to your family and society.
Just like the chicken night vision
If you are blind of knowledge
People will scorn and you will face hardship.
Have clear vision of future and don't lapse;
In your old age, don't be a subject to laughed at.

၁၆။

ဃရာဝါသ၊ သမ္ဗာဓဟု၊ ကိစ္စမြားမြောင်၊ လူတို့ဘောင်၌၊
အိမ်ထောင်သက်မွေး၊ ခြံနယ်မြွေးသား၊ လူ့ရေးကျယ်စွာ၊ အဖြာဖြာကို
လိမ္မာအတတ်၊ ချားရဟတ်သို့၊ လှည့်ပတ်ပြီးမှ၊ ကြိုတွက်ဆလျက်၊
လုံ့လပင်စည်၊ အရင်းတည်က၊ ခက်ရှည်ပညာ၊ ချမ်းသာအသီး၊
ကြီးစရှေ့ရှေ့၊ အခလေ့ဖြင့်၊ မမေ့မကျန်၊ လူမှုပွန်လျက်၊
စောင်မာန်မဲ့ဆုံး၊ တော်ဖြောင့်သုံး၍၊ နှလုံးသန့်စင် ကြယ်စေမင်း။ ။

16.
"A clan-household is a corporation,"[11]
Thus goes the saying.
Endless matters fill the human society.
Having family and livelihood,
Complex like a web of the termites,
Human affairs are wide, broad, and numerous. Be wise, skilled,
rounded, like a windmill. Think and plan well. Let your
industriousness be your capital investment.
Use your knowledge well so that prosperity
    and wealth will steadily grow;
Keep up with the disciplined life;
Do not neglect the social duties;
Have no pride or prejudice;
Be knowledgeable and honest;
Let your heart be clean and shine like a star.

---

[11] "ဃရာဝါသ၊ သမ္ဗာဓ"; Gharana (Pali) means 'clan' and Vamsa (pali) means
'family'. Sambādha (Pali) means 'pressure', 'crowding', 'inconvenience', 'narrow'.

Translated and explained by Shwe Lu Maung

၁၇။

လေးကျွန်းထိပ်ခေါင်၊ မြင်းမိုရ်တောင်နှင့်၊ ချိန်ဆောင်နှိုင်းလည်း၊
အတိုင်းမသိ၊ ကျေးဇူးရှိသည်၊ အမိကားတိုက်၊ သိုက်ကားမယားး၊
သားကားနွယ်ဆက်၊ ခက်လက်မျိုးဆွေ၊ ကျွန်ခြွေရွှေနှင့်၊
အုပ်တွေမကွဲ၊ လူခပဲအားး၊ ဆင်းရဲဖျောက်ပယ်၊
ချမ်းသာကယ်ရှ၍၊ လူဝယ်လူကောင်း၊ ဖြစ်တော်ရှောင်းဟု၊
လူပေါင်းပြောပ၊ ချီးမွမ်းရလျက်၊ ကြောင့်ကြဘေားဘျမ်းး၊
ဖျောက်နိုင်စွမ်းသားး၊ စိတ်ဝမ်းဖြောင့်တန်းး၊
ရွှေခင်ပွန်းကို၊ ချစ်ပန်းနှံ့ မပြယ်စေနှင့်မင်းး။   ။

17.

At the center of the four Islands,
Mount Meru is the Peak.[12]
Even when compared with Mt. Meru,
Immeasurable is the glory of
        gratitude we owe to Mother.
Mother is the world;[13] Wife is the nest; Children are the lineage;
Relatives are the branches;
Slaves and servants are the supports.
All the people together form the clan.
Do not discriminate anyone.
Remove poverty and suffering from them;
Let there be peace and wealth.
Only then, you are the human among the humans;
Good and righteous;
People will talk and praise you.
If such a human is your friend,
With a straight mind and stomach,
Let there forever prevail
        the sweet fragrance of the love flower.

---

[12] Burmese concept of the universe. There are four Islands or planets, namely, the North, the South, the West and the East. Our Human planet is the Southern Island. The cosmic Islands, the sun and the stars revolve around Mt. Meru.

[13] There is a saying "Thaung Tite Sakra-walar" (သောင်းတိုက် စကြာဝဠာ), meaning "there are 10,000 worlds in the universe." Therefore, I here translate 'Tite' (တိုက်) into 'world'. 'Tite' in general means a brick or stone house.

၁၈။

စေ့မြေ့သိပ်သည်း၊ ရွေ့ရွေ့ဆည်းသော်၊
စရည်းအိုးခွက်၊ ကြီးစွာလျက်လျှင်၊ တံစက်ကျများ၊
ပြည့်သောလားသို့၊ ပျား၏နည်းထုံး၊ မှတ်ကျင့်သုံး၍၊
ခြခုံးတောင်ပို့၊ ဖို့သည့်ခြင်းရာ၊ လူလိမ္မာတို့၊
ဥစ္စာဆည်းထွေ၊ တတ်လှစေလော့။
ကြွက်သေတစ်ခု၊ အရင်းပြု၍၊ ကြွယ်မှုတတ်ဆုံး၊
သူဌေးထုံးကို၊ နှလုံးမူလျက်၊ ကြံစည်နက်၍
သူထက်လွန်ကဲ ကြွယ်စေမင်း။ ။

18.

Be meticulous and make regular saving.
The earthen jar, no matter how big,
Drop by drop, water can fill it up.
Likewise, learn and follow the way of the bees,
And the way the ants make the hills.
As such, the wise people must know
how to save and accumulate the wealth.
Remember the life of the wealthy man
who became rich with a dead rat.[14]
With this in mind, think and plan deep;
Make yourself the richest of the rich.

[14] The well known story tells us a poor man volunteered to dispose of a dead rat. Thus he got the dead rat free. He sold it to cat's owner with big profit. Thus, his business began and he became the richest man in the kingdom.

၁၉။

လုံ့လပညာ၊ လိမ္မာတတ်ကို၊ ဆင်စွယ်စုံသို့၊ ကိုယ်ယုံမြဲမြဲ၊
ကောင်းအောင်သံသား၊ လုပ်ကြံသေသတ်၊ ယောက်ျားမြတ်တို့၊
မှတ်သည့်အတိုင်း၊ ပြည့်လှိုင်းချမ်းသာ၊ စီးပွားရှာလော့။ ။
ပညာချို့တဲ့၊ လုံ့လမဲ့ဟု၊ ကဲ့ရဲ့သဂြိုဟ်၊ [၁၅] သူများဆိုလည်း၊
ကိုယ်ကိုမချစ်၊ အကျင့်ညစ်သား၊ အပြစ်ဖွဲ့ဖို့၊ လူသွမ်းတို့ကား၊
မည်သို့မသိ၊ ပျင်းရိရိလျှင်၊ ရှိသည်ကိုယ်ဖို့၊ ကုသိုလ်ပို့က၊
ငါတို့နေရာ၊ စီးပွားလာဟု၊ ကြမ္မာကိုချည်း၊ မှတ်ထင်ရည်းရှင့်။ ။
ကျင့်နည်းညံ့ဆုံး၊ သူပျက်ထုံးကို၊ နှလုံးမငြိ တွယ်စေနှင့်မင်း။ ။   ။

19.

Be industrious and educated; be wise and skilled,
Like a tusker elephant,
Grow confidence in yourself.
Strive hard to be good and strong;
Plan and act in precision and accuracy.
Having these characteristics,
A noble heart works to accumulate
    wealth and richness.
Upon the uneducated and indolent,
The people look down and criticize.
But, those who do not love themselves
    pay no heed.
They live in their dirty ways and actions.
They put the blame on others.
Such are the vain men.
With zero know-how, they are simply lazy;
"In myself, if luck is there, the wealth
    will come to me,"
They believe thus and depend
    wholly on Karma.
Most inferior are the ways of
    the characterless people.
Don't let your heart entangle
    in the inferior ways.

---

[15] ၁၅ The Burmese use of သဂြိုဟ် has many meanings and uses depending on
the context. It may mean action, treatment, and undertaking funeral, among
many. Also see Appendix-6, p 110

၂၀။

ကျောင်းတော်ခရီး၊ ၁၆ လမ်းမကြီး၌၊ ပင်ထီးပညောင်၊ မြစ်တစ်ထောင်နှင့်၊
မြားမြောင်ခက်လက်၊ ရွက်လည်းစိပ်စိပ်၊ စေ့စေ့သိပ်လျက်၊
ရိပ်လည်းမြိုင်မြိုင်၊ လေမနှိုင်လျှင်၊ ပွတ်ခိုင်သီးမှည့်၊ အပြည့်ကျေးငှက်၊
စားလျက်သောင်းသဲ၊ မှိဝဲလူဗိုလ်၊ ရိပ်ခိုအများ၊ ခရီးသွားတို့၊
နေနားပျော်ရွှင်၊ ထိုသစ်ပင်ကား၊ ဝင်လာသသူ၊ ခပ်သိမ်းလူကို၊
ဆာပူငြိမ်းအောင်၊ စီးပွားဆောင်သို့၊ လူ့ဘောင်ကောင်းကြယ်၊
လူ့ကိုကယ်လည်း၊ ထိုနယ်လည်းကောင်း၊ ဖြစ်တုံရှောင်း၍၊
မျိုးပေါင်းဆွေဝါး၊ လူ့အများကို၊ သနားကြင်နာ၊ စီးပွားရှာ၍၊
မေတ္တာမကင်း၊ မစခြင်းဖြင့်၊ ထံရင်းမှီကိုးကွယ်စေမင်း။   ။

20.

On the journey to the Temple, on the highway,
A huge Banyan tree, with one thousand roots;
Numerous branches and sub-branches;
Covered with thick leaves, layers after layers;
The shade is cool and the wind
    cannot win the tree.
Ripe fruits in bundles on every branch;
Filled with countless birds, feeding and singing;
People and soldiers take rest under its shade;
The wayfarers take shelter,
    relax and enjoy there.
To everyone who comes under it,
The tree gives shade from the sun,
Makes them cool and happy.
Likewise, for the benefit of the society,
Being a person of wealth and strength;
To the friends, relatives, and people;
With kindness,
With the wealth you have,
With love and helping mind,
Let yourself be the host and shelter.

---

[16] ၁၆ ကျောင်းတော်ခရီး (On the journey to the Temple): for the explanation,
see the Appendix-4, p 107.

၂၁။

ပျူပျူငှာငှာ၊ လူတကာကို၊ သာသာချိုချို၊ ချစ်ဖွယ်ဆိုရှု၊
စိုစိုပြည်ပြည်၊ ချစ်မှုနည်နှင့်၊ လည်လည်ပတ်ပတ်၊ လောကဝတ်၌၊
ပြတ်ပြတ်သားသား၊ အပြားပြားလျှင်၊ မှုများခပ်သိမ်း၊
ဆောင်တိုင်းငြိမ်းလျက်၊ သူစိမ်းသူကျက်၊ ပေါင်းဖက်သရွေ့၊
မိဘတွေ့သို့၊ မွေ့မွေ့လျော့လျော့၊ ပျော်ပျော်ပါးပါး၊ နှုတ်ချိုပျားနှင့်၊
ဝတ်စားပေးပုံ၊ ပြည်းဖြူးနဲ့လျက်၊ အလွံ့ကျွန်ကျေး၊ ဆွေသားမြေးကို၊
ကျေးမွေးမညှိုးငယ်စေမင်း။   ။

21.

Be friendly and welcoming, to everybody.
Sweet and gentle, speak lovely.
Bright and cheerful, nurture lovely manners.
Be knowledgeable and understanding,
In the societal ways and manners.
Be clear and precise in all matters.
Make peaceful ending in every case.
Stranger or friend, when you meet,
Make it good as though
        you meet your parents;
Happy with light heart,
Let your words be sweet like honey;
Provide them clothing, food, and shelter.
Treat the same to your slaves, servants,
    friends, relatives, children,
    and grandchildren.
Do not let them feel small or neglected.

JၣJ"

လောကသာရ၊ ကျမ်းအစဥ့်၊ ဆုံးမစကား၊ မျိုးလေးပါးတို့၊
မှတ်သားစိမ့်ငှာ၊ ပျို့လက်ာဖြင့်၊ နည်းနာထွေပြား၊
လုံးပေါင်းကြားသည်၊ တခြား ပထမ တပိုင်းတည်း॥ ॥

22.

In this treatise of 'the Essence of the World',[17]
Are the advisory words
        to the four kinds of people.[18]
Making easy to learn by heart,
In the form of poetic stanza,
Presented are the ways, the manners,
        the disciplines, and the customs.
This is the end of Part 1.

---

[17] Laukathara
[18] Four kinds of people (အမျိုးလေးပါး), or four classes are (1) the Royals, (the king, including all his employees), (2) the ponna (the Brahmin or intellectual), (3) the well-to-dos (landlords, traders, business community), (4) the commoners (workers, small farmers, farm laborers, and subsistence traders).

Translated and explained by Shwe Lu Maung

လောကသာရ
ရခိုင်သူမြတ်

ဒုတိယပိုင်း
မင်းဆုံးမခန်း

Laukathara
Rakhine Thu Mrat

Part 2
Advice to the king

Translated and explained by Shwe Lu Maung

၂၃။
ပြည်သူ့ထွတ်ဦး၊ ဘုန်းရောင်မြှူးသည်၊ ရန်ဂူးလူ့ဘောင်၊
ထွတ်ခေါင်ရာဇာ၊ ဆုံးမနာလော့။
မဟာသမ္မတာ၊ ခတ္တိယတို့၊ နေကျကျင့်ရိုး၊ (၁) ကောင်းကျိုးအလှူ၊
(၂) စွန့်ကြမူလျက်၊ (၃) စိတ်ဖြူဖြောင့်စင်း၊ (၄) နူးညံ့ခြင်းနှင့်၊
(၅) သီတင်းစောင့်စည်း၊ (၆) မျက်နည်း (၇)သည်းခံ၊ (၈) ခြိုးခြံသမှု၊
(၉) မပြုညှဉ်းဆဲ၊ ဆင်းရဲမရှာ၊ မေတ္တာပွားဖြန့်၊ (၁၀) လူအဝန့်အား၊
မဆန့်ကျင်စေ၊ ဤသို့ရေသား၊ ဆယ်တွေစောင့်ကြပ်၊
တရားကွပ်၍၊ လက်ယပ်ခေါ်ပြု၊ သင်္ဂြိုဟ်မှုလည်း၊
လေးခုအစွေ၊ ပြကတွေဖြင့်၊ ကျင့်လေ့မကြွင်း ကျန်စေမင်း။   ။

23.
Oh King,
You are the head of the people.
Brilliant with glory,
Leader of the society -
Listen to my advice!
These are the laws followed and practiced,
By the First King Thamada of mankind and Kshatriya:
1. Charity with good virtue,
2. Self-sacrifice for benefit of others,
3. Service with honesty and sincerity,
4. Deal with humility and humbleness,
5. Observe the codes of morality,
6. Absence of hatred,
7. Practice tolerance,
8. Uphold austerity,
9. Avoid torture, and
10. Respect the public opinion.
Uphold these ten laws
    of King's precept.[19]
Welcome everyone with due humility,
With four friendship rules;[20]
Don't be negligent; don't make an exception.

---

[19] For the ten codes of king's precept, see the Appendix-5, p109
[20] For the four friendship rules, see the Appendix-6, p 110

၂၄။

ပြည်ကြီးသနင်း၊ မင်းဟူသည်ကား၊ ကြံစည်သူထက်၊ ဆယ်ဆတက်ရှ၍၊
အိပ်စက်နည်းပါး၊ လူအများကို၊ စီးပွားချမ်းသာ၊ နေ့တိုင်းရှာလျက်၊
အခါခပ်သိမ်း၊ မုဒိမ်းခိုးသူ၊ မပြုစေရ၊ ဆုံးမကွပ်ညှပ်၊
ပညပ်မလွန်၊ ရှေးမင်းမွန်တို့၊ ညွှန်ခဲ့သောတိုင်း၊ ကျင့်သမိုင်းဖြင့်၊
နှုန်းနှိုင်းမယွင်း၊ တမျဉ်းခင်းသို့၊ ကျင့်ခြင်းမချွတ်၊
တည့်မတ်မတ်လျှင်၊ လူနတ်ချစ်ဖွယ်၊ ကျေးဇူးကြွယ်လျက်၊
ကျင့်နွယ်လမ်းရိုး မှန်စေမင်း။။ ။။

24.

The head of a country,
A king must think and plan ten times
    more than others, and sleep little.
For peace, wealth and benefit of the people,
Every day must find ways and means.
At all times, robbery and rape
    must be prevented.
Advisories and education
    must be in place.
Punishment must not be extreme.
Follow the guidance of
    the earlier good kings.
Practice the well-established laws.
As a matter of comparison,
Let it be like a measuring tape;
Act straight and unbend.
Thus shall you earn the love of human
    and heavenly beings.
Always be beneficent, and
Follow the straight and right path.

၂၅။

မမေ့မလျော့၊ မပေါ့လုပ်ကြို၊ ကျွန်ကိုယ်ရံလည်း၊ မြဲမြဲစောင့်ရှောက်၊
ထက်အောက်တွင်းပြင်၊ မွမ်းဖျင်အပြည့်၊ အိပ်ဖန်ထည့်လျက်၊
အကြည့်အရှု၊ အမှုမသင့်၊ အကျင့်မကောင်း၊ အဟောင်းအသစ်၊
ထွက်ဝင်စစ်၍၊ ကျွန်ချစ်ကျွန်ယုံ၊ ထမ်းကိုမှုများ၊ ရေးခြားမြော်မြင်၊
တိုင်ပင်ကြိုသီး၊ အမတ်ကြီးကို၊ အနီးထံပါး၊ လက်စောင့်ထားရှို၊
ယုံမှားမဲ့လျှင်း၊ နှလုံးသွင်းလျက်၊ ချစ်ခြင်းသူ့ထက် လွန်စေမင်း။ ။

25.
Don't be negligence.
Don't be light in planning and action.
Always Keep the bodyguards,
Everywhere, upper and lower levels,
    inside and outside;
Ensure that every corner is covered.
Station night guards at your
    sleeping quarters.
Keep an eye on the watch and patrol.
Determine regular or irregular.
Distinguish good from bad.
Mark the new and the old.
Check the arrival and the departure.
Take into your service only those
    who love you and whom you trust.
Having deep and far sight,
Fruitful in planning and consultation,
Let such Ministers be near you;
Keep them handy.
Avoid misunderstanding,
Build confidence through your heart.
In this way, show that your love is
    beyond comparison.

၂၆။

ပြည်တဲ့အရေး၊ ပေါက်နှင့်ကျေးသို့၊ ကြံတွေးလှည့်ကာ၊ မသိသာတည့်။
ရေးရာထင်မြင်၊ မဖြစ်ခင်က၊ တိုင်ပင်မပြတ်၊ ကျွန်မှူးမတ်နှင့်၊
ကျမ်းတတ်ဟူးရား၊[21] တတ်မြောက်မြားသား၊ ပုဏ္ဏားရဟန်း၊
ရှေ့တွင်ဝန်းရှိ၊ ကိန်းခန်းတသာ၊ အခါမေးမြူ၊ ကောင်း၏ဟူလည်း၊
ကျင့်မှုမမွေ၊ အဓလေ့ဖြင့်၊ အရှေ့အနောက်၊ တောင်မြောက်ရေကြည်း၊
စီစစ်သည်းလျက်၊ စောင့်စည်းရိုတား၊ ကင်းသေထားရှိ၊
မြေခြားသူ မလွန်စေနှင့်မင်း။   ။

26.

The country affairs are like "Pauk and Kyey."[22]
It is hard to tell which is which.
Before the affair advances to a crisis,
Consult with the ministers.
Conference with the Ponna and Monks,
Who know the Books[23] and astrology.
Take their advice of astrological time
        and action.
Don't neglect the tradition.
Be firm in customary practices.
Everywhere, east, west, south, and north,
Station the army and navy.
Maintain a well-planned defense system.
Keep a force of scouts and intelligence.
Make sure that no foreign invasion occurs.

---

[21] ၂၀ ဟူးရား (Pali: होरापाठक) horāpāṭhaka, an astrologer.

[22] For the explanation, see the Appendix-7, p 111

[23] The Books are referred as "Kyan' (ကျမ်း) in Myanmar. They refer to the Vedic
literature and knowledge.

၂၇။

သူ့ပြည်သူ့ရွာ၊ သူ့ရပ်မှာဒ္ဂျိ၊ ခြင်းရာသိကြောင်း၊ တချောင်းချောင်းလျှင်၊
ညှံ့ပျောင်းရောဝင်၊ တိုင်ပင်ကြံ့ထွေ၊ သူလျှိုစေ၍၊ မနေစုံစမ်း၊
ကြိုးပမ်းလုပ်ဆောင်၊ အားအန်ထောင်လျက်၊ နောက်နောင်မြေးသား၊
စီးပွားစဉ့်ရှည်၊ တည်စိမ့်သောကြောင်း၊ နှုတ်ကောင်းခွန်းသာ၊
လက်ဆောင်စာနှင့်၊ စေပါစင်းလျင်း၊ ထိုထိုမင်းကို၊ ချစ်တင်းမေးမြန်း၊
ဆွေခင်ပွန်းဟု၊ မိတ်မှန်းကိုယ်ကို၊ တံတစ်ဆို၍၊
ချစ်လိုစကား မှန်စေမင်း။ ။

27.

In the foreign country,
In the foreign village,
In the foreign land,
Ongoing affairs and matters must be known;
Always keep awareness.
Implant the soft spies,
Who are miscible and crafty.
Collect the intelligence,
And the information in real time.
Strive for strength, peace and prosperity,
Lasting long, generation after generation.
With good and pleasant words,
Send envoys to many kings.
Enter into friendship and alliances.
Maintain friendship with felicitations and greetings.
Prove that you are a good friend;
Be true to your words of friendship.

၂၈။

ကိုယ့်ပြည်ကိုယ့်ရွာ၊ ကိုယ့်ရပ်မှာ၌၊ ဇာတာအလို၊
ကြိုဟ်လည်းမကောင်း၊ ထပ်လောင်းတိတ်ထံ၊ ပြတုံကျေးငှက်၊
နှုတ်ထွက်စနည်း၊ နှောင့်ယှက်သည်းမှု၊ စောင့်စည်းရိတား၊ မန္တရားနှင့်၊
သမားကွယ်ကာ၊ လွတ်စိမ့်ဝှာလျှင်၊ ကြိုဟ်စာလည်းပေး၊ သရွှေးပူဇော်၊
သကြိန်ခေါ်ရှို၊ သုံးဖေါ်မြတ်စွာ၊ ရတနာကို၊ မကွာကပ်ဆည်း၊
ကောင်းမှုချည်းလျှင်၊ ဖျင်ပည်းပြောထူ၊ စွန်.ကြိလ္လ၍၊
ကြည်ဖြူစိတ်ထက် သန်စေမင်း။ ။

28.

In your country, in your village,
   in your land;
Consult your birth stars.
If the constellations are bad,
With the evil signs and omens;
If the bird behaviors are irregular;[24]
If the 'opinion-voices' indicate troubles;[25]
Work to prevent and stop the disturbances.
Operate the 'Mantra'.[26]
Put the medicine men into action.[27]
In order to free from the danger,
Give food to the Planetary Spirits.[28]

---

[24] Burmese believe that the bird behavior may indicate good or bad fortune.
Scientifically, it is established that bird and animal behavior can be the indicator
of the weather and climate conditions, which in turn would determine the
agriculture. The ancient people developed a system of weather and climate
prediction based on the bird behavior, which became part of the Vedic astrology.
[25] The 'opinion-voices' or 'Sa-nae' (စနည်း) is a form of the talk of the town and
villages. "Listening to the voices of opinion" is a form of prudent gathering
and interpretation of the public opinion. The people, even in today's
Myanmar, express their opinion secretively due to fear of the authorities. In
the old days and also today, the kings and authorities operate the 'informers'.
[26] 'Mantra' is the verses of sacred words, which are believed to have mystic and
magical power.
[27] This is to prevent or stop the epidemic of the diseases that may come with the
bad 'Constellations'.
[28] For the explanations of the planets and spirits, see the Appendix-8, p 111

Perform 'Thandae Puja';[29]
Undertake 'purification'.[30]
Worship the 'Three Jewels'[31] without lapses.
Do good to acquire merits.
Give charity and donate plenty.
With high spirit,
Keep your mind clean and white.

၂၉။

ခပ်သိမ်းပြည်သူ၊ လူရဟန်းကို၊ သိမ်းမြန်းပိုက်ထုပ်၊
ကြက်သားအုပ်သို့၊ မလှုပ်စေကြောင်း၊ ဖြည့်ဖြားယောင်းလျက်၊
ကျင့်ဟောင်းမလွန်၊ တုတ်ခွန်မပြင်း၊ သနားခြင်းဖြင့်၊
နှိပ်နင်းကလူ၊ မပူစေရ၊ ကွပ်ဆုံးမလော့॥
ထွန်းပပြောင်ပြောင်၊ ထက်မိုးခေါင်၌၊ အရောင်ချမ်းလွန်၊
လဝိမာန်လျှင်၊ ပူပန်မရှိ၊ ငြိမ်းစေဘိ၍၊ ကြယ်တိရံကာ၊
တင့်တယ်စွာသို့၊ ပမာပုံသင့်၊ လနယ်ကျင်၍၊ လင်းပွင့်တိုင်းကား၊
စည်ပင်ပွားလျက်၊ လူများကောင်းချီး တွန်စေမင်း॥   ॥

29.

All the people, human and monks,
Keep them under your care and protection,
In the way the mother hen protects
        her baby chicks.
Do not give a chance of rebellion;
Meet the people's needs and bring them
        into your fold by persuasion.
Follow the standard rules and regulations.
Do not impose high taxation.
Be kind and allow no oppression.
Ensure there exists no concern or worry.
Give advice and oversee to these ends.
Bright and radiant, up in the sky,

---

[29] For the explanation of Thandae Puja, see the Appendix-9, p 113
[30] The 'purification' includes shampooing and washing hair with sacred ointments while reciting the 'mantra', and taking bath with the sacred Ganges water.
[31] The Three Jewels are Buddha, Dhamma, and Sangha.

Lovely and serene,
The heavenly Moon makes the world
    worry-free and peaceful;
It rules the stars, with splendor.
In the same manner,
Act and practice like the moon.
Be open and transparent.
Make the country grows and prospers.
Let the praise of people echo around you.

၃၀ ။

လူတို့အထိပ်၊ စိုးမိုးနိုပ်သား၊ တံဆိပ်မွန်ကင်း၊ မင်းတို့သည်ကား၊
ဖွေနည်စီစစ်၊ ရန်အမြစ်ကို၊ တူးပစ်နိုင်စေ၊ ရန်မြစ်သေမှ၊
ရှာနေပြည်သူ၊ ခပ်သိမ်းလူတို့၊ မပူမဆာ၊ ငြိမ်ချမ်းသာအံ့ ။
မလာနှစ်ဆစ်၊ မိုးကြိုးပစ်သို့၊ ရန်စစ်တို့ကို၊ ဖျောက်လွင့်ဖြိုလော့ ။
ရန်လိုမရှည့်၊ ရဲစွမ်းပြည့်သား၊ မလှည့်ခဲ့စောင်း၊ သူရဲကောင်းကို၊
များကြောင်းဆည်းပူး၊ ပေးကမ်းကြိုးလျက်၊ ကျေးဇူးအလိုက်၊
သိမ်းမြန်းပိုက်၍၊ ချစ်ကြိုက်သနား၊ ရင်၌သားသို့၊
ပြည်ဖြားမင်းရေး ပွန်စေမင်း ။   ။

30.

At the top of the people,
The ruler, the governor, and the controller,
The insignia and the pinnacle,
All in all is the king.
It is the king's duty,
To find, discover, dig out, and kill
    the roots of danger.
As such, all over the country,
You must ensure peace to the people,
Free of worries and concerns.
Do not let the dangers re-emerge;
Like a thunderbolt,
Destruct and destroy the warring enemies.
Ready to fight,
Brave and strong,

Determined and decisive,
Such are the heroes.
Grant them abundance.
Provide them generously.
According to the service,
Honor and place them in the right positions.
Love and care them like your own sons.
Be skillful in your delivery of kingship.

၃၁။

ကာမဒေဝ၊ စသည်အပြား၊ နတ်လေးပါးတွင်၊ တစ်ပါးမည်မှတ်၊
လောကနတ်ဟု၊ လူ့ထွတ်ဦးစွန်း၊ ဘုန်းတော်ထွန်းသား၊
လျှံဝန်းစိုးပိုက်၊ မင်းသို့လိုက်၍၊ ပြည်ခွဲပြည်သူ၊ မင်းအတူလျှင်၊
ကျင့်မှုမလွဲ၊ သုံးစွဲလေ့လာ၊ ကျင့်ကုန်ရာရှင့် ။
ရာဇာပြဓာန်း၊ ကြဎန်းမှန်ကင်း၊ အကြောင်းရင်းတည်း။
မင်းလျှင်တစ်ယောက်၊ လုံမစောက်ဖြင့်၊ မကောက်မယွန်း၊
တော်ဖြောင့်တန်းက၊ ထက်ဝန်းဗိုလ်ပါ၊ လူတကာလည်း၊
ညီညာတော်မှန်၊ မင်းအဟန်သို့၊ ကောင်းမွန်ကျင့်မှု၊ နှလုံးပြအံ့။
ပြည်သူ့မျက်ပွင့်၊ ကောင်းအောင်ကျင့်လော့။
ပုံသင့်ကျမ်းလာ၊ ဥပမာကား၊ အရာအထောင်၊ နွားကုန်အောင်တွင်၊
ရှေ့ဆောင်နွားလား၊ ဖြောင့်ဖြောင့်သွားသော်၊ နွားများစဉ်ဆိုက်၊
ဖြောင့်ဖြောင့်လိုက်သို့၊ စရိုက်ကျင့်မှု၊ ခပ်သိမ်းလူတို့၊
ထိုတူလည်းကောင်း၊ ဖြစ်ရာရှောင်သည်၊
မင်းကောင်း တော်ဖြောင့်မှန်စေမင်း။   ။

31.

Kāma Deva,[32] of them, are four kinds;
One kind called Loka Nātha,
Is the title of the king,
Because he is the leader of the people.
Thus, he is enshrined with honors
    and glorified with colors.
Accordingly, a king must not lack

---

[32] For the explanation, see the Appendix-10, p 113

codes of conduct.
Study, learn, and act well.
The Institute of the King is the pinnacle;
It is the Supreme Law.
If a king is like a lance,
Straight and unbendable;
The rank and file, and the people,
Will stay straight and united,
They will act like the king,
Good and well from their hearts.
O'pupil of the people's eyes,
Strive to be good and act well.
A parable in the Book says thus:
The cattle, in hundreds and thousands,
Among them is the Lead Bull;
If the Lead Bull goes straight,
All the cattle follow straight.
The same rule applies for the people.
Setting it as a model,
Be a good king, straight and righteous.

၃၂။

မာသုကုဇ္ဈိ[33] မဟာရာဇ[34] မာသုကုဇ္ဈိ ရထေသဘ[35]
သမ္ဗုဒ္ဓ လျှင်[36] ဆုံးမဟောထား၊ ဤတရားကို၊ မှတ်သားလည်းပြု၊
သည်းခံမှုဖြင့်၊ ပြည်သူ့ခမည်း၊ မျက်တော်နည်းလော့။
ချုပ်တည်းအမျက်၊ ထွက်လည်းမပြင်း၊ လူခပင်းကား၊ မင်းကိုဟူက၊
လောင်ပူရဲရဲ၊ ရားမီးခဲသို့၊ ဝမ်းထဲချဲ့ချဲ့၊ အမျက်မဲ့လည်း၊
တုန်လှဲသည်းချာ၊ ကြောက်လန့်ရှာ၏။
ပြင်းစွာအမျက်၊ ထွက်တပြီးကား၊ ကြက်သီးထဝုန်၊ အူချာမွန်မှု၊

---

[33] ၃၃ မာသုကုဇ္ဈိ (Pali: मा सु कुज्झि) mā su kujjhi: It is good not to get angry.

[34] ၃၄ မဟာရာဇ (Pali: महाराज) maharaja: Great King

[35] ၃၅ ရထေသဘ from (Pali: रथ) ratha: chariot; (Pali: सोभा) sobhā : beauty,
splendor, magnificence. Ratha sobhā: the magnificent one on the chariot. 'Lord
of Chariot' is my translation.

[36] ၃၆ သမ္ဗုဒ္ဓ (Pali: सम्बुद्ध) sambuddha: the Awakened or Enlightened one by
self-found knowledge.

အလွန်အကျူး၊ ကြောက်မိန်းမူးလိမ့်။

ဆူးဆူးရားရား၊ အမျက်အားကို၊ တရားချုပ်ကိုင်၊ မဆည်နိုင်လည်း၊
စိတ်ခိုင်တည်တံ့၊ ဆင်ခြင်င့်၍၊ မဝံ့နှစ်ဆစ်၊ ကြိမ်ဖန်စစ်လျက်၊
အပြစ်အလျောက်၊ သုံးကြိမ်မြောက်မှ၊ သေလောက်လျော်ဘေး၊
မင်းဒဏ်ပေးသည်၊ ကွပ်ရေး မများစေနှင့်မင်း။   ။

32.

"Great King, it is good not to get angry,
O'Lord of Chariot, it is good not to get angry,"
Thus said, Lord Buddha, the Awakened One.
Take his advice into your heart,
'Father of the People',
Keep your anger at the lowest.
Even when a king has anger controlled,
People at large are afraid of the king.
As though a burning ember dwells
    in their stomach,
They burn with fear.
If a king gets angry,
The goose pimples spring up in the people;
Their intestines twist and tremble;
They faint and stun with great fear.
Sharp and piercing like a thorn,
Anger is hard to control.
Even the law may not
    assist you check the anger.
Still then, keep your mind cool and steady;
Consider and wait;
Think and analyze repeatedly.
If found guilty,
Let there be a chance to repent;
Only when one commits a crime
    for the third time,
You may hand down the death penalty.
Thus, ensure that
    the executions are not common.

၃၃။

ခပ်သိမ်းပြည်သူ၊ လူတို့ထိပ်မိုး၊ ရေမြေစိုးသည်၊ ပြည့်ဖြိုးချမ်းသာ၊
မင်းတကာတို့၊ ကျင့်ရာအပြား၊ ခုနစ်ပါးလျှင်၊ စီးပွားစင်စစ်၊
များစွာဖြစ်၍၊ ရှင်ချစ်ဘုရား၊ မင်းတို့အားကို၊ ဟောထားခဲ့သည်၊
ခုနစ်မည်ကား၊ (၁) လူ့ပြည်စောင့်တတ်၊ နတ်ကိုမြတ်နိုး။ (၂)
အမျိုးဆွေနိုး၊ သက်ကြီးရှိသေ။ (၃) ပြည်နေရွှာသူ၊
နိုင်ငံထက်မူဖြင့်၊ မယူသားမြေး။ (၄) မှုရေးတိုင်ပင်၊ (၅)
ညီညွတ်အင်နှင့်၊ (၆) လာကျင့်ထက်ဝန်း၊ ရဟန်းပုဏ္ဏား၊
သိမ်းပကားရ၍၊ တရားမယွင်း၊ ဖြည့်တင်းမွေးကျွေး၊ မလာသေးသော်၊
နီးဝေးရပ်သား၊ သူတို့အားကို၊ မသွားစေအောင်၊ ကျေးဇူးဆောင်လျက်၊
(၇) ပြည်ထောင်စိုးကွပ်၊ ပညပ်မလွန်၊ လမ်းမှန်စိုက်စိုက်၊
ရာထပ်လိုက်လျက်၊ တိမ်တိုက်လှစ်ထွန်၊ လအဝန်းသို့၊
လေးကျွန်းရိပ်မှောင်၊ ဘုန်းအရောင်ဖြင့်၊ ပြောင်ပြောင်ဝင်းဝါ၊
ငြိမ်ချမ်းသာ၍၊ ပြည်ရွာတိုင်းကား၊ ပွားစေမင်း။ ။

33·

Among all the people,
On the top of all human,
Ruler of the water and land,
Rich and powerful,
Such kings must follow seven rules of law,
Prescribed by the loving Lord Buddha.
The seven rules of law are:

1. Love the Nātha[37] who guards the human world;
2. Respect the relatives and aged people;
3. Do not violate or force a woman to be your wife;
4. Consult with the ministers and people in all matters;
5. Strive for unity;
6. Welcome and take into your fold of the monks and ponnas who come to you, with due respect and justice. Feed and supply them well. To those, far and near, who have not yet come to you, give good benefit so that they

---

[37] Burmese believe that the throne, the king, the crown, the country, the world, the universe, and every other thing are guarded and protected by the guardian angels (Nātha in Pali or Nat in Burmese).

do not depart you.
7.   Rule the country well; Do not be extreme in the law
     enforcement; Without deviation, follow the right path.
As such, like the moon that shines through the thick cloud, drive
away the darkness of the world. With your radiant virtue, make
it bright and shine. In a peaceful environment, all over the
country, village, and province, let prosperity prevails.

၃၄॥

သမ္ဘာ^{၃၈} ရင့်ဖြိုး၊ ရှေးကောင်းကျိုးကြောင့်၊ တန်ခိုးထွန်းလျှို၊
လူထိပ်စံသား၊ ဘုန်းချွန်ရန်နည်၊ မင်းတို့သည်ကား၊ အရှည်ရေးရာ၊
မြင်နိုင်စွာသား၊ လိမ္မာတတ်သိ၊ ပညာရှိကို၊ ပီတိချစ်ပြင်း၊ နှလုံးသွင်း၍၊
ဆိုခြင်းထွက်သံ၊ နားပါးခံလျက်၊
ထုံးစံနည်းနာ၊ တိုင်ပင်ရာ၏။ ၃ဍာဏ်ဝါ ထွန်းမြူး၊
ဂုဏ်ဖြင့်ထူးသား၊ ကျေးဇူးရောင်ညီ၊ ပညာရှိနှင့်၊ ပြည်ကြီးသနင်း၊
ပြည့်ရှင်မင်းတို့၊ မကင်းစေရာ၊ ဥပမာကား၊ ရတနာမြရှု၊ နန္ဒမုဋ္ဌိ၊
မဣ္ဍပန်လား၊ ကျော်ထင်ရှားလျက်၊ နှစ်ပါးပေါင်းဖက်၊
အကျိုးနက်အံ့॥ ထမ်းရွက်ဆောင်ပြု၊ ပြည်တဲ့မှုကြောင့်၊ စေ့ငုမြင်ပြီး၊
ပညာကြီးကို၊ နည်းတီးထုံးရှေး၊ ပုံစံမေး၍၊
ကျင့်ရေး လွန်စိပ် ပြားစေမင်း॥   ॥

34.
Bestowed with the accumulated merits of virtue, from the good
actions of the past lives;
With the flaming might,
At the top of the people,
The powerful and the conqueror is a King.
Such a king must love the Wise Persons,
Who see afar,
Who know the knowledge.
Take them into your heart;
Consider what they say;

---

[38] ၃၈ သမ္ဘာ (Pali: सम्भार) sambhāra: requisite ingredients, accumulation.
 Sanskrit: सम्भर, sambhāra: bestower, one who brings together, supporter, great
gorgeousness.

Give ear to them;
Consult in all matters of strategies and tactics.
Radiant with intelligence, distinguished
    with honors, loyal and faithful;
With such Wise Persons and the King,
    who is the owner of the country,
Must not be separated.
This, here, is the established parable.
Only in the jewel jade Cave of Nandamu (Happiness),[39]
The Myitzu Flower blooms to its fame.
The two in their companionship
    brings deep mutual benefit.
Likewise, for the sake of the country,
The Wise who sees all and each,
Must be consulted in all matters of strategies and tactics.
Make sure that you act with a broad and open mind.

၃၅॥

ဆင်မြင်းရထား၊ ခြေသည်အားနှင့်၊ လေးပါးစစ်အင်၊ စတုရင်လည်း၊
မွမ်းဖျင်ဖြီးတွေ၊ များလှစေလော့॥
အနေမကျ၊ ရန်စစ်ထသော်၊ ဖြဖြလိုက်လံ၊ စစ်ဦးနှံမှ၊ ရှိလေရှိ့ရှိ့၊
နောက်မဝှဲ့တည့်॥ ဖိုရှိ့ညည်းတည်း၊ ကြောက်လန့်သည်းရှို၊
သရည်းလေဘွယ်၊ ရန်စစ်ပြယ်လိမ့်॥
မပြယ်လေသီး၊ စစ်မက်ကြီးမှု၊ ပွန်းတီးမှုဆောင်၊ သူရဲခေါင်ကို၊
ဆင်ပြောင်မုန်ဖပ်၊ မင်းစီးအပ်ရှို၊ နောက်တပ်အများ၊
ဆင်မြင်းပြားလျက်၊ ရှေ့ဖျားလည်းတင်၊ စစ်စီရင်လော့॥
စစ်ဆင်သုံးပါး၊ အများဖြီးထပ်၊ ပွင့်ချုပ်ကြာသွင်၊
ဆင်လည်းချွန်းတည်း၊ မြင်းလည်းဇက်ချုပ်၊ ခြေသည်အုပ်လျက်၊
စက်ရုပ်အဝန်း၊ ကော့ယွန်းထွက်ဟန်၊ လှည်းသဏ္ဌာန်သို့၊
တတ်ပွန်နားဝင်၊ စစ်ရေးဆင်ရှို၊ အောင်မြင်စိမ့်တွေ၊ ဥပဒေဖြင့်၊
စစ်မြေအရပ်၊ စစ်မှူးကွပ်လျက်၊ ရှုပ်ရှုပ်ထိုးခုတ်၊ ကြက်ရဲစုတ်သို့၊
အားထုတ်လွန် ကြိုးစားလေမင်း॥ ॥

---

[39] For more information on the jewel jade Cave of Nandamu (Happiness) and Myitzu Flower, see the Appendix-11, p 114

35.

Elephants, horses, chariots, and foot-soldiers,
Four forces of the military power;
Keep them regimented and combat ready,
Trained, skilled, and numerous.
If unsettled and war breaks out,
Move quick and fight on the front,
With gallant and valor, show the might,
So that the enemy won't
     dare to challenge again.
Then will the war end.
If unaccomplished and the war intensifies,
Appoint a brave hero in the command.
Give him your best military elephant,
Recruit more forces, elephants, and horses;
Sent them to the front and wage the war.
Effectively apply three military tactics.[40]
Operate the Lotus Operation;
Attack with the layers after layers of soldiers.
Coordinate the Elephants, Horses,
    and Foot-soldiers for the Circle Operation.
Plan and command well
    for the Flanking Operation,
Advancing like the curvature of a wheel.
With wisdom and skill,
Conduct the military strategies.
In view of victory,
Let there be law and discipline.
In each battlefield, post a Field Commander.
Fight with the lightening speed;
Like the kite swoops down on the prey,[41]
Put great effort and strive hard.

---

[40] Three military tactics are (1) Lotus, (2) Circle, and (3) Flanking Operations, as described in the poem.
[41] The chicken is figured as a prey in the poem.

Translated and explained by Shwe Lu Maung

၃၆။

သာမျ⁴²၊ မစ္စ၊⁴³ စသည်အင်္ဂါ၊ ခုနှစ်ဖြာကို၊ ပြည်ရွာပြကတွေ၊
စုံစေ့လျှင်းအောင်၊ ပြည်တဲ့ဆောင်သည်၊ ပြည်ထောင်ဟူက၊
ပြည်ကိစ္စကို၊ လုံ့လဖြိုးထူ၊ နှလုံးမူလော့။
ရန်သူကြောက်ဖွယ်၊ နက်ဒွမ်းကျယ်သား၊ ပင်လယ်ကျိုးမြှောင်း၊
ရေနေကောင်းလျက်၊ ရဲလောင်ရင်တား၊ တံခါးတူရိုင်၊
ကြံခိုင်မြို့ကို၊ တစ်သိန်းဖြိုလည်း၊ မပြိုနိုင်မှု၊ ကြီးကျယ်ထုနှင့်၊
မျက်ရှုလှုတင့်၊ တန်ဆောင်းဆင့်၍၊ သွယ်မြင့်ပြဆောင်၊
မြှားမြှောင်လက်နက်၊ မြို့ထက်ပတ်လျှောက်၊ စစ်တဲ့ဆောက်၍၊
ရင်လျှောက်ပတ်ကုံး၊ သူရဲဖုံးက၊ စသည်မကျန်၊ တမ်းခွန်လောက်လွဲ၊
စူးရဲအစ၊ အနေကျလျှင်၊ သဗ္ဗကိရိယာ၊ မြို့တန်းဆာလည်း၊
များစွာပြည့်နက်၊ ကုံစေလျက်လျှင်၊ ကြမ်းခက်ရဲမာန်၊ ခြေသော့ဟန်သို့၊
ရန်ကိုကဲမိုး၊ မိုးနှယ်ကြိုး၍၊ တန်ခိုးကျော်ထင် ရှားစေမင်း။ ။

36.

The King, the ministers are parts of the
seven features of a kingdom.[44]
Keep these features well and strong,
Across the country and villages.
In a country, the country affairs
    must live in your heart, with all due care.
Fearsome to enemy, like an ocean,
The moat must be wide and deep.
The drawbridge and the gate must be solid and strong.
With embrasures and merlons,
Massive and broad must be the city wall,
That one hundred thousand men
    could not break it down.
Strong and beautiful,
Magnificent towers must be built,
With the splendor of tall and high spires.

---

[42] ၄၂ သာမျ (Pali: सामी) sāmī : lord, master, owner, husband.

[43] ၄၃ မစ္စ (Pali: अमच्च) amacca : minister, councilor.

[44] Seven features of a kingdom capital are 1. King, 2. Ministers, 3. Sovereignty, 4. Fortified Capital, 5. Wealth, 6. Military, and 7. Allies, as per description of Min Thuu Wun's Laukathara Pyo, p 146.

Having numerous weapons,
The military stations and
   the soldier-walk[45] must be
   all around the city;
The brave-hide[46] must be constructed well.
Slings and catapults must be in place;
Spikes and sharps must be well positioned;
The banners and flags must be flying;
All kinds of machinery must be equipped.
Thus shall the features of the city must be complete and abundant.
Fearless and ferocious, like a lion;
High above the enemy, like a thunderbolt;
Make your power travels far and wide.

၃၇॥

အမျိုးလေးပါး၊ ပုဏ္ဏား ပုဏ္ဏေး၊ သူဌေးသူကြွယ်၊ ကုန်သွယ်စည်ပင်၊
သူထင်သူရှား၊ ပြည်နေများလျှက်၊ စပါး ရေ ဆန်၊ အလွန်ဖျင်ပြဲ၊
ပြောင်းပဲလူးဆပ်၊ အထပ်ထပ်လျှင်၊ အလပ်မြေနည်း၊ လုပ်ကြံဆည်းမှ၊
ပစ္စည်းဖျင်ဖြီး၊ ပြည်ကြီးလက္ခဏာ၊ ရေစာလောက်ငံ့၊ စေ့နှံ့သိုထား၊
ဆေးသမားနှင့်၊ ဟူရားမကွာ၊ တတ်လိမ္မာသား၊ ရေးရာပွန်းတီး၊
မတ်ကြီးကြံထက်၊ တုံးသက်တိုင်ပင်၊ မြော်မြင်ကျိုးကြောင်း၊
ခင်ပွန်းကောင်းလည်း၊ တိမ်းစောင်းယိမ်းမပ်၊ စောင့်မကွပ်လျှက်၊
ထူထပ်တိုင်းကား၊ များလေအောင်လျှင်၊ ပြည်ထောင်နေမျိုး၊
လုပ်ဆောင်ကြိုးလော့॥ မြင်းရိုးဆင်သည်၊ စစ်ကျင်လည်သား၊
ခိုင်ကျည်သူရဲ၊ ရန်မဖဲကို၊ ဆကဲမြတ်လေး၊ ကျေးမက်ပေးရှို၊
သိမ်းမွေးဖြည့်တင်း၊ ဖြန့်ဖြူးခြင်းဖြင့်၊ လွန်မင်း ချစ်သနားစေမင်း॥   ॥

_____

[45] The path on the top of the city wall; wall-walk.
[46] Battlement or a place built on the wall-walk for the defensive ambush.

37.

Four kinds of people[47] are there.
The Ponna, Ponnae,[48]
Millionaires and rich people,
Big and famous traders and business people,
must love to live in your country.
Paddy, water, rice must be plenty.
Corn, legumes, barley, sorghum,
Must grow multiple crops.
Do not keep a land empty, uncultivated.
Only then, there will be abundance of food.
Befitting to a great country,
Water and food must be sufficient for all.
Store the extra.
Medicine men, Hora astrologers,[49]
Skilled and expert, learned and knowledgeable,
        are the wise ministers,
Keep them well and consult with them unto death.
They know and they see;
They are good companions.
With them, keep the country straight on the right path.
You, the Founder of the country,
The descendant of the Sun,
Strive to have many of them.
Horsemen and elephant-men,
Skilled in warfare;
The braves who are strong,
        disciplined, and daring;
Give them care and respect;
Grant them rewards and awards;
Treat them as your family;
Help them prosper and develop.
As such, you shall show your love and kindness.

---

[47] Four kinds of people (အမျိုးလေးပါး), or four classes are (1) the Royals, (the king, including all his employees), (2) the ponna (the Brahmin or intellectual), (3) the well-to-dos (landlords, traders, business community), (4) the commoners (workers, small farmers, farm laborers, and subsistence traders).

[48] Ponnae is a woman Brahmin or intellectual.

[49] ဟောရာ: (Pali: होरापाठक) horāpāṭhaka, an astrologer.

၃၈။

အခေါင်ကြုခုန်း၊ လူ့ထိပ်ထွန်းသား၊ ဦးစွန်းအချာ၊ မင်းတကာတို့၊
ပမာပုံခင်း၊ ခြေသေ့မင်းနှင့်၊ ကျင့်ခြင်းတပြေ၊ တူကြစေလော့။
လေးထွေအရှိ၊ ခြေသေ့မျိုးတွင်၊ တန်ခိုးကြီးခေါင်၊ တောသုံးထောင်ကို၊
စိုးဆောင်နိုပ်နင်း၊ စွမ်းအားပြင်းသည်၊ သားမင်းမြတ်စွာ၊
ကေသရာလျှင်၊ အခါန်စွ၊ သဘာဝဖြင့်၊ သူရသတ္တိ၊ ရဲခြင်းရှိ၍၊
မိမိအစာ၊ ရှာလိုခါ၌၊ နေရာကျောက်ဂူ၊ ထွက်လတ်ပြူသော်၊
တူရှုရှုကြည့်၊ မလှည့်ငဲ့စောင်း၊ ခြိမ်းမောင်းသုံးခွန်း၊
မွန်းမွန်းဟောက်သံ၊ မြူးတူးစံမှ၊ ချုံချုံစိုက်စိုက်၊ သားကိုလိုက်၍၊
သတ်ကိုက်စီးနှဲ့၊ သွေးသံသောက်တုတ်၊ အားအန်ထုတ်၍၊
ကိုက်ဆုတ်နိုပ်နယ်၊ ကြီးငယ်မဟူ၊ ဖမ်းကာယူသို့၊ လူတို့ထိပ်လယ်၊
စိုးစံပယ်သည်၊ ဖုန်းကြွယ်ရာဇာ၊ ကျင့်အပ်စွာ၏ ။
ရေးရာမျှော်ရှု၊ ခပ်သိမ်းမှု၌၊ ဗဟုကိစ္စ၊ ဟူသမျှကို၊
လုံ့လပြင်းထူ၊ အားကြီးမှုဖြင့်၊ ရန်သူခပဲ၊
ဝေးစွာရဲ၍၊ ပြည်တဲ့ပွင့်လင်း သာစေမင်း။   ။

38.

The crown and the throne,
The supreme of the people,
The vertex and pinnacle,
Are the kings.
In this parable, you are advised to act
     like the lion king.
Among the four kinds of lion,[50]
Kethara, the ruler of
     the three thousand jungles,
The most powerful and strong,
Is the Lion King.
By nature, he is brave and
     courageous at all time.
When he hunts for food,
He emerges from his rocky cave;
With his head straight,
With his eyes focused forward,
With grace, he roars three times,

---

[50] For the four kinds of lion, see the Appendix-12, p 115

Loud and echo far and wide.
Then, he marks the prey;
Chases it resolute and determined;
Kills and subdues with powerful bite;
Big or small, he sucks the blood
    and consumes the meat.
Likewise, must act a king,
The supreme ruler of the people.
In all affairs,
In all concerns,
Investigate every aspect;
Be industrious;
Make great effort;
Keep away all and every enemy.
Let your country be free and peaceful.

၃၉॥

နာရာဓိပတိ၊^{၅၁} သိဒ္ဓိ^{၅၂} ထွန်းတင်၊ မြတ်ဆုံးတင်သည်၊
ပြည့်ရှင်ဖုန်း^{၅၃} လှိုင်း၊ ပုံနည်းခိုင်း၍၊ ဥပျိုင်း၄ုက်တူ၊
ကျင့်တော်မူလော့॥
ဖြူသည်အဆင်း၊ မွေးရောင်ဝင်းသား၊ လည်ပင်းခြေရှည်၊
ထို၄ုက်သည်ကား၊ ဖွေနည်အစာ၊ လှည့်ပတ်ရှာသော်၊
မြစ်သာမြစ်လောင်၊ ချောင်းမြှောင်ကမ်းနား၊ သွားလားမွေ့ညက်၊
ငြိမ်သက်ကဏ္ဍဖွေ၊ ကြည့်ထွေရှုစိန်း၊ မိန်းမိန်းနေလျက်၊
ရေမပွက်ကျင်၊ ငါးကိုမြင်သော်၊ ခုံမင်လျှပ်လျှပ်၊ မိအောင်ခွပ်သို့၊
ပြည်ကွပ်လူမှူး၊ စောရန်ၚူးလည်း၊ စူးစူးကျင့်မူ၊ ဗျိုင်းအတူလျှင်၊
ဟူဟူသရွေ့၊ အခလေ့ဖြင့်၊ မမွေ့စောင့်ရှောက်၊ သာလျောက်ဖြည့်ဖြည့်၊
ကျင့်သိပိသည်းလျက်၊ တိုင်းတည်သမူ၊ မျှော်ကြည့်ရှုမှ၊ အန်တုအန်ပ၊
ရန်ထိုမျှကို၊ အစထောၚ်လော်၊ ပေါ်သည့်အကြိုက်၊ ကွပ်ညပ်လိုက်၍၊
နောက်ၚ္၍ ရန်မလာစေနှင့်မင်း॥   ॥

⁵¹ ၅၁ နာရာ (Pali: नर) nara: man, a human being. အဓိပတိ (Pali: अधिपति) adhipati:
Lord, chief, sovereign, master.

⁵² ၅၂ သိဒ္ဓိ (Pali: सिद्धि): siddhi; Formation, accomplishment , success, prosperity.

⁵³ ၅၃ ဖုန်း पुञ्ञ (Pali: पुञ्ञ): puñña ; merit, righteousness.

39.

The Chief of the people,
Honored with accomplishment,
The noblest of all,
The Righteous Lord of the country;
As a matter of model,
You must act like an egret.
Radiant with white feathers and plumes,
Graceful with long neck and legs,
In its search for food,
It roams about the rivers and creeks,
Stands motionless with grace,
Looks and searches with good focus and concentration.
When a fish is sighted,
It strikes and grasps with precision.
Likewise, the defender of the country,
The chief of the people,
Conqueror of the enemies,
Must act with grace and skill, like the egret.
In all matters,
Establish a code of conduct;
Be steady and cool;
Be patient and focused;
Analyze all the cases brought before you.
When a challenge is in view,
When an enemy emerges,
From the very beginning,
Fight and eliminate effectively;
Make sure no recurrence can occur.

၄၀॥

ဗာဟုဗလ၊ စသည်တွက်ရေ၊ အားငါးထွေကား၊ᴼᴼ ရေမြေသနင်း၊
မင်းတို့ဉ့်သာ၊ ပြည့်နိုင်ရာဟု၊ မြတ်စွာဘုရား၊ သုံးလူ့ဖျားလျှင်၊
ဟောကြားမိန့်မြွက်၊ ရွှေနှုတ်ထွက်ဖြင့်၊ မယွက်စေအောင်၊
ကျေးဇူးဆောင်လော့॥

လူ့ဘောင်လူ့ထွတ်၊ လူမင်းမြတ်တို့၊ ဆင်မှတ်တန်းဆာ၊ ရတနာသို့၊
မကွာမြဲတည်၊ အားငါးမည်တွင်၊ အထွတ်တင်သား၊ မျက်ရှင်အလား၊
ပညာအားလျှင်၊ စီးပွားမြင်နိုင်၊ အခေါင်တိုင်၏॥ ပြည့်လိုင်ကျေးဇူး၊
အထူးထူးတွင်၊ အမှူးစင်စစ်၊ ရှေ့သွားဖြစ်လျက်၊ အပြစ်ခွါရှောင်၊
အကျိုးဆောင်သား၊ တတ်ခေါင်ပညာ၊ မတ်လိမ္မာကို၊ စေပါသုံးစွဲ၊
ကိုယ်ဉ့်မြဲက၊ ငရဲမလား၊ ရှေးရှုသွားလျက်၊ မြတ်ဖျားနိဗ္ဗာန်၊
ခရီးညွန့်ရှင့်॥

သမန္တစက်၊ᴵᴵ အမြင်နက်သား၊ ပွားတက်ပညာ၊ မတ်လိမ္မာကို၊
ဆရာတစ်ဆူ၊ တိုင်ပင်မူလျက်၊ ဆုံးမခက်သား၊ သူပျက်သုံးယောက်၊
ပါယ်မကြောက်ကို၊ နှင့်ခြောက်ခြိမ်းမောင်း၊ စီးတစောင်းလျှင်၊
ထောင်းထောင်းညက်ညက်၊ မျက်နှာဖျက်ရှို၊
ရန်ဘက် မညှာတာစေမင်း॥   ॥

40.
Five kinds of prowess are there, beginning with the physical
prowess.[56]
The Five Prowess[57] are attainable
Only by the kings,
Said Buddha, the Lord of Three Men,[58]
From his golden lips.
Therefore, gratify his words without failure.

---

[54] ၅၄ See the Appendix-13, p 116, for the Five Prowess (အားငါးထွေကား).

[55] ၅၅ သမန္တစက် (samantacak) from Pali: समन्ता, samantā: all around,
everywhere; and चक्खुमा, cakkhumā: Having eyes or sight , seeing; having
supernatural insight or wisdom

[56] ဗာဟုဗလ (Pali: बाहु bāhu; बल; bala) the strength of arm, physical prowess.
Also see Appendix-13, p116
[57] See the Appendix-13, p116, for the Five Prowess.
[58] Three Men are the peoples of (1) human world, (2) Nat Devata world, and (3)
Brahma world.

Leader of the people and society,
King of the people,
Like the jewelry you wear,
Do not part with Five Prowess.
Among the Five Prowess,
The Prowess of Knowledge is the Third Eye,
Most magnificent above all.
Among many benefactors,
It is the lead and the chief.
Like a wise minister,
It helps you avoid mistakes;
It brings you good tidings.
If you apply and use it at all time,
If you keep it with you at all time,
You will not go to hell.
It will advance you toward
      the noble path of Nibban.[59]
The deep insight known as Samantacak,[60]
Is the prosperous knowledge.
Take it as a wise minister.
Worship and consult it as a teacher.
Impossible to tame are the Three Bad Entities,[61]
That are not afraid of hell.
Drive them away.
Inflict fear into them.
Destroy and crush them all.
Make them lose face.
Don't show kindness to these enemies.

---

[59] Nibban is Pali and Nirvana is Sanskrit for Enlightenment.

[60] သမန္တစက် (samantacak) from Pali: समन्ता, samantā: all around, everywhere; and चक्खुमा, cakkhumā: Having eyes or sight , seeing; having supernatural insight or wisdom

[61] သုပျက်သုံးယောက် (the Three Bad Entities) are

(1) လောဘ, (Pali: लोभ: lobha): greed, covetousness; (2) ဒေါသ, (Pali: दोस: dosa): anger, corrupting, defect, fault; and (3) မောဟ, (Pali: मोह: moha): stupidity, delusion .

Translated and explained by Shwe Lu Maung

၄၁။

အပ္ပမေယျ၊[62] အနန္တ[63] လျှင်၊ ဆုံးစမထင်၊ ကမ်းမမြင်သား၊
ရေပြင်ဝန်းကျယ်၊ ပင်လယ်မြစ်မ၊ သမုဒ္ဒ[64] ၌၊ ငါးရာငါးစင်း၊
မြစ်ခပင်တို့၊ စင်းလျှင်းမချာ၊ စီးဝင်လာသို့၊ ချမ်းသာခေါင်ရောက်၊
မင်းဖြစ်မြှောက်က၊ ထပ်လျှောက် ရတနာ၊ များလှစွာသား၊
ဥစ္စာရွှေငွေ၊ အထွေအပြား၊ အပါးပါးလျှင်၊ ဝတ်စားတန်းဆာ၊
လိုရာရာတီ၊ မကြာမတင်၊ ရောက်လာလျှင်လည်း၊ လိုချင်သမျှ၊
မပြုလေကျင်၊ ပြည်ကြီးရှင်တို့၊ ဆင်ခြင်ကောင်းစွ၊ စိတ်လောဘကား၊
တစ်ရာတစ်စင်း၊ ထီးဆောင်မင်းကို၊ လက်ရင်းကြုပ်သို့၊ ကျွန်ပြုလိုရှင့်။
သို့ကိုသော်လည်း၊ နည်းသည်နှင်နှင်၊ လိုအင်ပြည်ခဲ၊ မရောင့်ရဲတည့်။
ပြည်တဲ့သနင်း၊ မင်းတို့ဖုန်းအား၊ စည်ပင်ပွားရှ၍၊ ပြည်သားပြည်သူ၊
ပြောထူပစ္စည်း၊ ဖျင်ပြည်ခိုင်ဖြိုး၊ ကွယ်မြောက်ပြီးမှ၊ သစ်သီးခိုင်ပြွတ်၊
မှည့်မှဆွတ်သော်၊ ကောင်းမြတ်ရသာ၊ ချိုမြိန်စွာသို့၊ ပမာထို့ဟန်၊
မှည့်ခါတန်မှ၊ တုတ်ခွန်ခိုင်ပြွတ်၊ ပြည်သီးဆွတ်လော့။
ထိမ်းမှတ်မင်းစား၊ တစ်ချို့ထား၍၊ အများကျွေးမွေး၊ ဝေငှပေးသည်၊
ကျင့်ရေးတတ် လိမ္မာစေမင်း။ ။

41.

Immeasurable, endless and infinite,
No land in sight,
All but water,
Meeting point of the rivers,
The ocean is wide and broad.
Into the ocean,
Five hundred and five rivers,
Without failure, flow in.
Likewise, on the crown of the good fortune,
When you become a king,
Piles of jewels will come to you in abundance.
Treasure, gold, and silver of many kinds,
Whatever you want,

---

[62] ၆၂ အပ္ပမေယျ (Pali: अप्पमेय्य, appameyya):
immeasurable.

[63] ၆၃ အနန္တ (Pali: अनन्त, ananta): endless; limitless; infinite.

[64] ၆၄ သမုဒ္ဒ (Pali: समुद्द, samudda): the sea; ocean

Will be in your possession without delay.
However, do not encourage your desire;
The Lord of the country must act with control.
The King of the one hundred and one kings,[65]
The Greed will tempt you to be its slave.
No matter what, if discontent rules you,
You will long for more wealth and glory.
However, be mindful of the people;
Only when the people are prospered,
The king can be prospered.
Let the people be rich and prosper,
Like a tree full of fruits.
Let the fruits be ripe and well,
Sweet and pleasing, bearing the good taste.
Then, you may reap your royal tax.
Keep some for your treasury;
The rest you must distribute
        among the people,
For their welfare and development.
As such, you must act wisely.

၄၂။

ဝသုန္ဓရာ၊[66] မြေမျက်နှာထက်၊ သမ္မာရင့်ဖုန်း၊ ကုသိုလ်မှုန်းၡို၊
ချိန်ဆုန်းခါသင့်၊ ပန်းနယ်ပွင့်သား၊ ရင့်သည့်တေ၏၊[67] တန်ခိုးပသည်၊
လူများမျက်စိ၊ နရာဓိ[68] တို့၊ ဂတိလေးပါး၊[69] မမှားစေအောင်၊
ကျေးဇူးဆောင်လျှက်၊ တည်ထောင်ကမ္ဘာ၊ အစစ္စကာ၊ ဆရာမန၊
ရသေ့ပြုသား၊ လူမှုဆုံးဖြတ်၊ ဓမ္မသတ်[70] နှင့်၊ ညီညွတ်မယွင်း၊

---

[65] A common Burmese expression of the king of the kings. Every Burmese king
is referred in this way.

[66] ၆၆ ဝသုန္ဓရာ (Pali: वसुन्धरा, vasundharā): The earth; an epithet for the
Enricher or the Bearer of Treasure.

[67] ၆၇ တေ၏ (Pali: तेज): teja; heat; radiance; glory; power

[68] ၆၈ နရာဓိ (naradhi), a word synthesized from Pali: नर; nara; man; a human
being and Pali: अधिपति; adhipati; lord; master; ruler, meaning the lord of men
or king.

[69] ၆၉ See the Appendix-14, p 116 and also Footnote 72.

[70] ၇၀ ဓမ္မသတ် see footnote 74.

စောင့်စည်းခြင်းဖြင့်၊ မပင်းမျက်နှာ၊ မနာအားပါး၊ နှစ်ဖက်သားး၏၊ အကြားတည့်မှန်၊ ချိန်ခွင်ဟန်သို့၊ ဇကန်ကျကျ၊[71] မေးမြန်းမှလျှင်၊ ဆဆတွေးတွေး၊ ရှုးနိုင်ပေးလော့။ အရေးအလျောက်၊ မပေါက်မပြန်၊ ကျမ်းဒ္ဓိညွန်သား၊ ရှေးလွန်နည်းမှိုး၊ ထုံးတီးမှုတ်သား၊ ပိုင်းခြားအဟုတ်၊ စက်သွားခုတ်သို့၊ စုတ်စုတ်တွင်းတွင်း၊ ကြိုထိုးထွင်းရှု၊ စင်းစင်းမတ်မတ်၊ တရားဖြတ်သည်၊ လူနတ်ကောင်းချီး ၁ြာစေမင်း။ ။

42.

On the surface of the earth,
Enriched with all virtues and merits,
Like flower that blossoms at the right time,
Highly radiant with power,
A king is the eyes of people and
The Lord of the human.
You must act not to violate the Four Gati,[72]
But bring forth the benefit to the country.
From the day of the origin of the world,
Teacher Manu,[73]
Wrote down the Laws, Dhammathet;[74]
You must follow his laws in all human affairs.
Avoid favoritism.
With no hesitance,
You must stand
Unswayed, right in the middle,
Like a balance, with one mind.[75]
Ask and hear all the words of the concerned.
Investigate and think.
Only then, you may give your verdict.
See the factuality of the case.

---

[71] ၇၁ ဇကန်ကျကျ See Footnote 75.

[72] See the Appendix-14, p 116, for the explanation of Four Gati (ဂတိလေးပါး).

[73] Teacher Manu is the author of the Laws of Manu. In Burmese records, Manu was a Ra-the (Pali: इसि; isi ; A ṛishi, a saint, a sage, a holy man) at the beginning of the humankind. However, in the Hindu sacred texts Manu has different meanings.

[74] ဓမ္မသတ် (Dhammathet) is the Burmese version of Sanskrit (धर्मशास्त्र) Dharmaśāstra. Here it is the Laws of Manu.

[75] With one mind (ဇကန်ကျကျ) means without any confusion.

Without deviation from
   the guidance of the Book,
Maintain the ancient traditions.
Based upon the rules and regulations,
Like an action of a machine,
Thorough and proper,
Apply your wisdom and intelligence.
Then, give the verdict straight and righteous.
You must earn the praise of heaven and human.

၄၃။

မဟီပတိ၊[76] ယသသိ[77] ဟု၊ မြေကြီးသခင်၊ စည်းစိမ်ဖျင်သား၊
ကျော်ထင်လူ့ပြည်၊ မင်းကြီးသည်လျှင်၊ အရှည်မမျှော်၊
မတော်မလျား၊ မွေ့လျော့ငြားရှု၍၊ တရားမစောင့်၊ မဖြောင့်မစင်း၊
အကျင့်ယွင်းမှု၊ ထိုမင်းလက်ထက်၊ မြေကြီးလျက်လည်း၊ သက်ခဲ့သြဇာ၊
အောက်မှာရွှေ့လေ၊ ထဲနက်ဗွေ့ဒို၊ နေဘိရကား၊ အများပည်းဖျင်၊
ရောက်လှည့်ကျင်သား၊ သစ်ပင်သစ်သီး၊ မကြီးလုံးဖန်၊ အမွန်ရသာ၊
သြဇာမရှိ၊ ပျက်သိသိတည့်။
ထိုပြီးအပ၊ ဆေးဝါးစသည်၊ တေဇမထ၊ ပျက်ခဲ့ရသာ၊ စားလေပါလည်း၊
အနာလွတ်ခဲ၊ ရွှေ့ရွှေ့ကဲလျက်၊ ကောင်းမြဲမကောင်း၊
မိုးလည်းအောင်ရှု၍၊ သောင်းခဲ့ကောက်ပင်၊ မျိုးမရှင်တည့်။
ပြည်ရှင်မင်းကြီး၊ တရားမှီးမှု၊ မြေကြီးရသာ၊ သြဇာတိုးတက်၊
ချိုမြက်သစ်သီး၊ အကြီးလုံးလှ၊ ဆေးဝါးစသည်၊ တေဇထက်မြတ်၊
ရောဂါလွတ်၍၊ ရွှာလတ်မအောင်၊ ကောက်မသောင်းတည့်၊
မင်းကောင်းထို့ကြောင့်၊ တရားစောင့်လော့။
ရှစ်ထောင့်မြေပြင်၊ ရန်ကိုသင်လျက်၊ ပြည်တွင်ပြည်သူ၊

---

[76] ၇၆ မဟီပတိ: Min Thuu Wun explained it as a combination of Pali, မဟီ + ပတိ
(mahii + pati), meaning (earth + lord) or king, on the page 151 of his book.
However, I did not find mahipati or mahiipate in the Pali dictionary but I found
mahiipate in the Sanskrit dictionary that defines "महीपते (mahiipate): O King".

[77] ၇၇ ယသသိ: (Pali: यसस्सी, yasassī): Famous

ခပ်သိမ်းလူလည်း၊ ဆုယူများစွာ၊ ချစ်ကြင်နာ၍၊ မေတ္တာ⁷⁸ မိုးကို၊
ဖြိုးဖြိုးနေ့တိုင်း ရွာစေမင်း။ ။

43.

O'Famous King, the Lord of the Earth,
Having abundance of luxury,
The eminence of human world;
If the king acts without looking afar;
If the king acts improper,
With negligence and injustice,
Not straight but dishonest;
If a king acts wrong;
In his days,
The earth will move its nutrients
Deep down to its interior.
So will numerous trees and fruits
Become thin and small.
The taste will be lost and
The nutrients will decay.
In addition,
Medicinal herbs will become powerless;
Ineffective even though administered well;
Will not be free from the illness;
Bad will become worse;
Rain will also stop;
The crop will dwindle;
The seedlings will fail to grow.
When the King, Lord of the Land,
Stands on justice,
The essence of earth is rich with nutrients.
Sweet and wonderful are the fruits,
Beautiful and large in size.
The medicinal herbs and plants
Are potent and powerful.
Freedom from illness prevails.
In every village with no exception,
The crop seedlings grow healthy.
Therefore, O'Good King,

---

[78] ၇၈ မေတ္တာ (Pali: मेत्ता mettā): Friendliness; friendly feeling; good will;
kindness; love; charity.

Protect justice.[79]
In the eight corners of the Earth,
Eliminate the enemies.
In the country,
The people are numerous in many kinds. Provide them with
abundance of benefits,
So that they will love you with good hearts;
So that they will everyday shower you with Mettā good wishes.

၄၄။

လင်္ကာဒီပ၊ သီဟဠုဟု၊ နာမပြဓာန်း၊ သိန်းဃိုကျွန်းဒွဲ့၊
ထွန်းသည့်နေသွင်၊ တန်ခိုးထင်သား၊ သင်္ခဗောဓိ၊
အမည်ရှိသည်၊ မင်းကြီးကျင့်တူ၊ နှလုံးမှုလေ့။
နတ်လူချစ်ပြင်း၊ ထိုသည့်မင်းကား၊ စောင့်ခြင်းတရား၊
မယွင်းမှားတည့်။ ခိုးသားပူလောင်၊ ခေါင်သည့်မိုးနှင့်၊
နတ်ဆိုးဘီးလူး၊ စားကြူးလူသား၊ ဘေးသုံးပါးကို၊ သိကြားနတ်တိုင်၊
ဓိဋ္ဌာန်ခိုင်လျက်၊ အသက်စွန့်စား၊ ပြည်သူများကြောင့်၊
ဖိတားဖျောက်ပေ၊ မိုးကောင်းစေ၏။
ကျင့်ထွေထို့လား၊ မတတ်ငြားလည်း၊ ရှိုးရှားဆိုတောင်း၊
ကျိုးတစ်ကြောင်းမျှ၊ မင်းကောင်းရန်ကဲ၊ ကျင့်မှုရဲလေ့။
ဖေါက်လဲတတ်စွာ၊ သက်ခန္ဓာကား၊ အခါမြင့်ရှည်၊ မတည်နိုင်ဘူး။
ကျေးဇူးသော်မှု၊ လူ့ဘော်မြင့်ကြာ၊ ချီးမွမ်းရာလျှင်၊
ကမ္ဘာပတ်လုံး၊ ပြောမဆုံးတည့်။
ရှေးထုံးနည်းခိုင်၊ ကောင်းကျင့်လှိုင်ရှို့၊ လူတိုင်းအှုံ့အဲ၊
ချီးမွမ်းကဲလျက်၊ မြင့်မြကျေးဇူး ဖွာစေမင်း။ ။

---

[79] Compare this with the phrase "Dharmo Rakshati Rakshita" (Dharma protects who protects Dharma), Chapter 8, section 15 of the Laws of Manu and Mahabharata 3:311.

Translated and explained by Shwe Lu Maung

44.

In the land of Lanka Dipa,
Also known as Sinhala or Lion Island,[80]
Radiant like the sun,
Famed for prowess,
Sangha Bodi,[81]
Was the name of the great king;
Keep his codes of conduct in your heart.
He was greatly loved by Nāt[82] and Human;
He protects justice;
He never violates justice.
In his days,
There were three dangers,
The danger from criminals,
The danger from drought,
The danger from Satan, Ogre, and Cannibals.
In the witness of the King of Heaven,[83]
He fought the three dangers;
He risked his life,
In view of the people welfare.
With brave fight, he vanished the evils;
Brought about good tidings to his people.
Even if you cannot act that great,
Be a humble model,
Act well for the good cause.
O'Good King of Courage,
Be bold to act good.
Impermanent is this life and body;

---

[80] These names refer to Sri Lanka of today. Lanka was the name used in Mahabharata and Ramayana, great epics of ancient India. Sinhala is Sanskrit meaning the blood of lion as per Wikipedia article, http://en.wikipedia.org/wiki/Names_of_Sri_Lanka. Sinha or Singha are both Sanskrit and Pali for lion.

[81] Siri Sangha Bodhi I (r. 252-254 CE) also known Siri Sangabo was a king of Anuradhapura of ancient Sri Lanka as per http://en.wikipedia.org/wiki/Siri_Sangha_Bodhi_I_of_Anuradhapura. He is known even today as righteous king in Sri Lanka. His place of sacrifice, Attanagalla, is a popular tourist and pilgrim site.

[82] Burmese word 'nāt' (နတ်) is derived from Pali नाथ: nātha, which means protection or protector. In Burmese culture, nāt is a heavenly being or (pali: देवता, devatā): A deva, a celestial being, an angel, or a deity.

[83] သိကြားးနတ် (Thikra-nāt) is Burmese for Indra or Sakra of Indian religions.

It does not last long.
An act of gratitude though
Stays in the words of the people,
As long as the world lasts.[84]
There are ancient knowledge,
    treatise and codes.
Consult them and follow them well.
Let everyone, with great appreciation, shower praises upon you.
Thus shall you act
To earn high and lasting gratitude.

၄၅॥

သဟဿနေတ္တ၊[၈၅] ဝါသဝ၊[၈၆] ဟု၊ သက္က[၈၇] သူရိန်၊[၈၈] ဒေဝိန်[၈၉] နတ်ဖျား၊
မိုးသိကြား၊[၉၀] လျှင်၊ တရားစောင့်သူ၊ ကျင့်ကောင်းလူကို၊ ရေးယူစိမ့်ငှ၊
လေးမျက်နှာ၌၊ ကွယ်ကာရန်ထောက်၊ နတ်လေးယောက်ကို၊
စောင့်ရှောက်ပိုင်းခြား၊ အမြဲထားသို့၊ တိုင်းကားအုပ်စိုး၊
ပြည်ထိပ်မိုးသား၊ တန်ခိုးထွန်းလင်း၊ လူတို့မင်းလည်း၊
ကျင့်ခြင်းထို့တူ၊ ဆင်းရဲသူအား၊ ကလူညှင်းဆဲ၊ မခဲစိမ့်ငှ၊
ရုပ်မျက်နှာကို၊ ကွယ်ကာစိမ့်ကြောင်း၊ ကျင့်ကောင်းမွန်ရည်၊
သဘောတည်လျှက်၊ ကြံစည်နက်နဲ၊ မှုထမ်းရဲသား၊ ခက်ခဲရေးရာ၊
လိမ္မာတတ်မြောက်၊ မတ်လေးယောက်အား၊ လက်အောက်မှာထား၊
လေးဘို့ခြား၍၊ လေးပါးဒီသာ၊ ရုပ်ခန်းဝါ၌၊ ပြည်ရွာကိစ္စ၊ ဟူသမျှကို၊
ဆုံးမကန့်မြစ်၊ အပြစ်ပေးကောင်း၊ မပေးကောင်းဟု၊

---

[84] Compare this expression with "No act of kindness, no matter how small, is ever wasted," Aesop's Fables.

[85] ၈၅ သဟဿနေတ္တ (Pali: सहस्सनेत्त, sahassanetta): the thousand-eyed Sakka.

[86] ၈၆ ဝါသဝ (Pali: वासव, vāsava): the king of the gods

[87] ၈၇ သက္က (Pali: सक्क, sakka): the king of devas, Sakra or Indra. For example see Sakka-pañha Sutta: Sakka's Questions.

[88] ၈၈ သူရိန် (Thureen) a Burmese adaptation of Pali सूरिय (sūriya): the sun. A figurative expression referring to a king.

[89] ၈၉ ဒေဝိန် (Dewinn) a Burmese adaptation of Pali देवता (devatā): A deva, a celestial being, an angel, a deity

[90] ၉၀ မိုးသိကြား (Mo-Thi-Kya). Popular Burmese name for king of the heaven. Mo (heaven) + Thi ([all] knowing) + Kya [all] hearing).

အကြောင်းစုံစမ်း၊ ရှေးကျင့်တမ်းဖြင့်၊ မူထမ်းအနေ၊
ကွပ်ညှပ်စေ၍၊ လူ့မြေထွတ်ထား၊ လူမင်းဖျားလည်း၊ လေးပါးနတ်တူ၊
ပမာမူလျက်၊ ပြည်သူစောင့်ရှောက်၊ မတ်လေးယောက်နှင့်၊
အုံလောက်လူ့တောင်၊ ပြည်တဲ့ဆောင်၍၊
ပြည်ထောင်ကြောက် ရှ့ိရှားစေမင်း။ ။

45.

Armed with one thousand eyes,
The king of the gods,
Sakka,[91] radiant like the sun,
Is the ruler of the devatā.[92]
Sakka, All-Knowing and All-Hearing of the Heaven,[93]
Appoints and positions four Angels,
At four horizons,
Laden with the duty of the protection
        of those, who guard the law and
        who practice good actions.
Likewise:
The ruler of the vast land,
The highest umbrella the country,
Bright and radiant with power,
A human king must also act.
To the poor,
Exploitation and tortures must not come.
All over the country,
In view of guarding them well,
Appoint public servants and police,
Who possess:
Good characters, honest mind,
        skill and vision.
In order to tackle the difficult cases,
Wise and intelligent Four Ministers,
Must be at your immediate reach.
Keep four departments,
To rule the four directions of the country.
Let there be offices to discuss

---

[91] Also see the footnote 87, သက္က the king of devas.
[92] Also see the footnote 89, ဒေဝိန် a celestial being.
[93] Also see the footnote 90, မိုးသိကြား Popular Burmese name for king of the heaven.

The matters of the villages and country.
How to right the wrongs,
Punish or not to punish,
All matter must be investigated.
Weigh with the treatise and codes of the past.
Towards this end,
There must be officers appointed.
Thus shall be your administration.
The crown of the human world,
The king, the head of the people;
Following the example of the four Angels,
For the protection of the people,
Four ministers, you must have.
To the wonder of the humanity,
When you rule the country well,
The other kingdoms
Will not dare challenge you.

၄၆။

အခါတစ်ပါး၊ မြင်းမိုရ်ဖျားဝယ်၊ သိကြားနေရာ၊ စစ်ထိုးလာသား၊
ပြင်းစွာမျက်ရှိန်၊ အသူရိန်ကို၊ ဒေဝိန်သက္က၊ စီးချင်းချ၍၊ ဒေဝသဘာ၊
သုဓမ္မာဟု၊ သာသည်စရပ်၊ အမိုးယပ်တွင်၊ နှောင်ကြပ်အမြဲ၊
တုပ်၍ဆွဲသော်၊ ဆဲဆဲရေးရေး၊ ဟစ်ကြွေးရွေ့ရွတ်၊ တတွတ်တွတ်လျှင်၊
အပတ်တကုတ်၊ ကြမ်းကြုတ်စကား၊ နတ်မင်းဖျားကို၊ နွားနှင့်အတူ၊
ငရဲသူဟု၊ ကလူကစာ၊ ဆဲရေးရှာလျက်၊ မျက်မထွက်တည့်။
ဆိုဘက်မထိုက်၊ သင်းသူမိုက်ဟု၊ မှတ်ပိုက်သော့ထွေ၊ သည်းခံပေ၏။
ရွှေမြေရပ်စည်၊ ရွှေနန်းတည်သား၊ နတ်ပြည်သနင်း၊ သိကြားမင်းလျှင်၊
ခံခြင်းသည်းညည်း၊ အမျက်နည်းသို့၊ ရေကြည်းတောတောင်၊
အာဏာဆောင်သား၊ ဖုန်းခေါင်ထွန်းလင်း၊ လူတို့မင်းလည်း၊
ပုံခင်းကျမ်းလာ၊ ထိုကိုစာ၍၊ ပြင်းစွာအမျက်၊
မထွက်တို့ရာ၊ ချုပ်မြစ်ထာလော့။
ပညာတိုင်းတည်း၊ မျက်မာန်နည်းမှု၊ လူလည်းပြောဟော၊
နတ်ချစ်မောသည်၊ ကျော်စောကောင်းချီး ၄၁စေမင်း။ ။

46.

Once upon a time,
On the top of Mount Meru,
The Kingdom of Sakka was attacked,
    ferociously and strongly, by Asura.[94]
In the war, devatā Sakka won the duel;
He tied up Asura, and kept him hanging
From the roof of Sudhamma[95] Hall
Where the devatā assembles.
Asura yelled and abused Sakka;
He called Sakka a bull;
He called Sakka a Hell Warden;
He kept scolding and mocking Sakka.
However, with the mind that
    it does not worth to rebut a bad person,
Sakka took it easy without anger.
In the golden land of prosperity,[96]
The Lord of golden palace,
King of the devatā,
Sakka, was tolerant with least anger.
Likewise,
Over the water, land, forest, and mountains,
With authority enforced,
Powerful and radiant, the king of human,
Must learn the lesson from this canonic story.
Ferocious anger
    should not be allowed to come out;
Check and control it effectively.
With due wisdom,
When anger is kept lowest,
People will talk good of it;
Heaven will love you for it.
Therefore, your fame of goodness
    will travel far and wide.

---

[94] The war of Asura and Sakka (Śakra) is a popular Hindu and Buddhist mythology. You can find many credible articles on line.
[95] Thudhamma (သုဓမ္မာ) is Burmese transliteration of Sudhamma.
[96] This refers to Mount Meru where Sakka has his heaven.

၄၇။

လောကသာရ၊ ကျမ်းဂန္ထ၍၊ ဓမ္မရသာ၊ အလင်္ကာဖြင့်၊
တန်းဆာလည်းဆင်၊ ဖွဲ့စီရင်လျက်၊ ကျမ်းမြင်ထွေပြား၊
အပါးပါးနှင့်၊ များသည့်ထုံးနည်း၊ မှတ်ဖွယ်ချည်းတည့်။
ပမည်းပမာ၊ နည်းနာနယ၊ သွန်းပုံချသို့၊ ခတ္တိယရာဇာ၊ ဇနာဓိပ၊
ဘူပါလဟု၊ လောကထွတ်ဖျား၊ မင်းတို့အားကို၊ စီးပွားချမ်းသာ၊
ဖြစ်စိမ့်ငှာလျှင်၊ ပညာသေတ္တ၊ ရုံးစည်းပြု၍၊ ကျင့်မှုတရား၊
မှတ်စိမ့်ကြားသည်၊ တခြား ဒုတိယပိုင်းတည်း။ ။

47.

This is Laukathara (the Essence of the world),
A classic treatise,
The truth of Dhamma (the Laws),
With the poetic beauty.
Decorated and composed here are:
Different views of knowledge,
    from numerous books,
Many codes and regulations,
All are worthy of learning.
The examples are set;
The codes and the laws are described.
The Warrior[97] king,
The Lord of the people,[98]
Man of many strengths,[99]
Pinnacle of the world,
These are the advice for the kings of such.
For the enrichment of wealth and prosperity,

---

[97] The original word is khattiya (Pali: खत्तिय ခတ္တိယ): a man of the warrior caste; belonging to Khattiyas. Sanskrit: Kshatriya

[98] The original word is janadhipa (Pali: जनाधिप, ဇနာဓိပ). Jana: a person; a man; the people. Dhipa is from adhipa (Pali: अधिप: lord; master; ruler.

[99] The original word is bhubala (ဘူပါလ), which is combination bhu and bala. Bhu is from (Pali: भुस, bhusa): chaff; husks of corn; much; abundant. Bala is from (pali: बल, bala): strength; power; force; an army; military force.

The essentials of good knowledge[100]
    are collected and organized;
The codes of conduct are
    presented for your heart;
This then is the end of Part 2.

---

[100] The original word is pañña + suṭṭhu (ပညာ + သောဠူ). (Pali: पञ्ञा, pañña):
wisdom; knowledge; insight.

(Pali: सुठु, suṭṭhu; Well; exceedingly). According to Min Thuu Wun's translation,
page 168 of his book, သောဠူ (thetu, in Burmese writing and pronunciation)
literally means "oil and marrow". Nearest English translation will be "the core,"
"innermost value," "essence," or "the best."

လောကသာရ
ရခိုင်သူမြတ်

တတိယပိုင်း
ပုဏ္ဏားဆုံးမခန်း

Laukathara
Rakhine Thu Mrat

Part 3
Advice to the Ponna

၄၈။
မှတ်ကြကုန်လော့၊ ဗြဟ္မာ့နွယ်ရိုး၊ ပုဏ္ဏားမျိုးကို၊
ကောင်းကျိုးစကား၊ ငါလျှင်ကြားပိမ့်။
ရှေးဖျားကမ္ဘာ၊ အစစ္စကာ၊ ဗြဟ္မာပိုင်းခြား၊ ဆေးသမားနှင့်၊
ဟူးရားကြယ်မြင်၊ ကောင်းကင်နက်သတ်၊ တတ်သည်တသီး၊
ယစ်မီးပူဇော်၊ ဖြော်ဖြော်မန်းရွတ်၊ ကြိုဟ်နက်သန္တေး၊ ဦးဆေးတခြား၊
ခေါင်ဖျားဗေဒင်၊ သိမြင်နဲ့စပ်၊ တိဝိကပ်[101] နှင့်၊ ကလာပ်ဗျုဒ္ဓိ၊[102]
ဒဿဝိဒဂ်၊ ကျမ်းခက်ဗျာဂရိင်း၊ တတ်နိုင်းတခြား၊ လေးပါးကျ]သို့၊
ပုဏ္ဏားတို့တွင်၊ မချို့ကျေးဇူး၊ အထူးသမိုက်၊ မျိုးလိုက်မှတ်သား၊
ဆေးသမားလည်း၊ ဆေးဝါးတတ်ကျွမ်း၊ ပိဿ္စောပြွမ်း၍၊
ဆေးကျမ်းထိုထို၊ ရသာကိုလည်း၊ ဖွင့်ဆိုတတ်ကျယ်၊ ဓိပ္ပါယ်အနက်၊
လွန်လှေ့ကျက်၍၊ ဓာတ်ပျက်သည်းခြေ၊ သွေးလေချောက်ချား၊
သလိပ်များက၊ စသည့်ရောဂါ၊ အနာအမျိုး၊ ကိုးဆယ့်ခြောက်ပါး၊
အပြားပြားကို၊ မမှားလွတ်အောင်၊ ကုသဆောင်၍၊
အခေါင်သမား မြှောက်စေမင်း။ ။

48.

Record in your mind;
The descent of Brahma,
Oh Ponna People;
The words of benefit, I will speak.
Since ancient world, from the beginning,
The Brahma makes four disciplines,
(1) The Medicine;
(2) The Astrology that sees the stars,
And knows the sky and constellations;
(3) The Priesthood with authority to light

---

[101] ၁၀၁ Tivikat (တိဝိကပ်) means three intellectual treatises that refer to the three Vedic texts. Of the four Vedic texts, the Burmese honor the first three (1) Rig Veda, (2) Sama Veda, and (3) Yajur Veda. The Burmese consider the Atharva-Veda is false and unholy and do not use it. Also see Emil Forchhammer, *Report On The Literary Work Performed On Behalf Of Government During The Year 1879-80*, Nabu Press, 2012, page 11. Please do not confuse with the Buddhist Cannons that are called Tipitaka (Pali) or Tripitaka (Snaskrit).
[102] ၁၀၂ Sanskrit *Kalapa-Parisishta* Grammar Treatise.

sacrificial fire for puja, recite the mantra,
Perform Planetary Spirits and Thandae Pujas,[103]
Wash the hair and head; and
(4) The Veda, the study of
        three Vedic Treatise,[104]
The book of *Kalapa-Parisishta*,[105]
The writings of Dandin,[106]
The book of Vidagdha,[107]
The difficult book of the disciplines
Of poems and rhymes.
Thus, skilled, learned, and specialized are
        the four kinds of ponna.[108]
A medicine-man must know
All medical disciplines,
Including Bimdaw[109] medicine.
You must have deep knowledge
        of the medical systems,
Must be able to investigate and diagnose.
Always study;
Illness of the alimentary tract,
Disorders of the blood and wind,
Sickness of the respiratory tracts,

---

[103] See the Appendix-8, p 111 for the Planetary Spirits and Appendix-9, p 113 for Thandae Puja.

[104] See the footnote 101 for the Vedic Treatise.

[105] Sanskrit Kalapa or Katantra Grammar Treatise written by Kumara. See, for example, *A Descriptive Catalogue of Sanskrit Manuscript* in the Library of the Asiatic Society of Bengal, Culcutta.

[106] Dandin was a 7th or 8th century Sanskrit author who wrote poems or Kāvya (ကဗျ); See http://en.wikipedia.org/wiki/DanDin

[107] A book known as *sridharmadasasurikrtam vidagdhamukhamandanam* on the disciplines of poem by Dharmadāsasūri. For example see http://www.worldcat.org/title/sridharmadasasurikrtam-vidagdhamukhamandanam-candrakala-vyakhyaya-hindibhasanuvadena-ca-vibhusitam/oclc/644338053?referer=di&ht=edition

[108] Also see V9, p 7; V37, pp 36-37

[109] Burmese word Bimdaw (Bhesijja) refers to a branch of medicine that uses herbs and diet for the treatment. The Burmese medical system is comprised of the (1) Desana system, (2) Bhesijja (Bethitzza) system, (3) Nekhatta (Astrological) system, and (4) Vijjadhara (Vezzadara) system. See for example http://www.searo.who.int/entity/medicines/topics/traditional_medicine_in_unio n_of_myanmar.pdf   and http://www.burmalibrary.org/docs14/Traditional-Medicine-Handbook-Project-JICA-red.pdf

The ninety-six kinds of illness,
In all varieties,
You must be able to detect and treat well.
Make yourself the greatest medicine man.

၄၈။[110]

ဟောရဂန္ထ၊ ဂဏနဟု၊ သိပ္ပဟူးရား၊ တတ်မြှောက်မြားသား၊
ပုဏ္ဏားနွယ်ရိုး၊ သူကောင်းမျိုးတို့၊ ကြိုးကြိုးကုတ်ကုတ်၊
အားအန့်ထုတ်၍၊ အဟုတ်နေ့လ၊ နာရီစသည်၊ ကြားကသိတတ်၊
ဖြူဟုတ်ရာဇာမတ္တဏ်၊ ကိန်းဆန်ရူးဝန်း၊ ကြိုဟ်သွန်းမန်းကပ်၊
ထပ်ကြပ်အညီ၊ အသိတိစုတ်၊ ဖော်ထုတ်ဓာတ်ကျမ်း၊ ခွဲခြမ်းစိတ်ဖြာ၊
တတ်လေ့လာ၍၊ သတ္တာဗီသ၊ လှည့်ထနက်သတ်၊ မြင်းမိုရ်ပတ်သား၊
ဒွါဒသံရာသီ၊ ယာယီစက်ကွင်း၊ ကြိုဟ်နင်းကြိုဟ်ပြောင်း၊ ကောင်း
မကောင်းသား၊ ကျိုးကြောင်းဆုံးဖြတ်၊ လနေကြတ်နှင့်၊ ဉပ္ပါတ်အာယု၊
စဉ်းမှုတတ်ပွန်၊ စက်အဟန်သို့၊ ထုံးမွန်ကားကား၊ အသားအရိုး၊
စုံပြည့်ဖြိုးလျက်၊ ဟိုးဟိုးထင်သိ၊ ပညာရှိဟု၊ ကိတ္တိထင်ရှား၊
ဗြဟ္မဇ္ဇသားတို့၊ ဟူးရားတတ်ခေါင် မြှောက်စေမင်း။ ။

49.[111]
The Vedic Hora book, horā gantha,
The book of Number, gaṇanā;
Having the knowledge of
Such astrological science,
Are the Ponna.
The people of good family,
Strive and study hard,
Put in great effort.
When the day, the month, the hour,
Are known, you must know what to do.

---

[110] ၁၁၀ The meanings of the Pali words in this verse are given in
the Appendix-15, p 118. There are many Pali words in this verse.
[111] The meanings of the Pali words in this verse are given in
the Appendix-15, p 118. There are many Pali words in this verse.

You must know the texts of
Varāh, RajamataM, Kimcan, Dhuvan.
Skilled in calculating the ephemeris,
The planetary alignment, and
Prediction of the eclipse.
Using the eighty analytical methods,
Reveal and diagnose the elements.
Analysis and interpretation,
Must be your expertise.
The twenty seven planets
Revolve around Mt. Meru.
Know the twelve Zodiac Houses,
The planetary position and transition;
Is it good or bad?
You must be able to tell.
The solar and lunar eclipses
That may have dangerous impact on life,
You must be able to calculate.
Like a computer,[112]
You must be skilled and efficient.
You must be solid
Filled with flesh and bones.[113]
Let you be known and recognized.
With a note of learned,
Famous and distinguished,
Sons of Brahman,
Be a top expert in Vedic Astrology.

၅၀။

သာမယဗ၊ ကၠရဗေဒင်၊ သုံးပုံမြင်၍၊ သန့်စင်သီလ၊ အာစာရနှင့်၊
မိဘမျိုးစစ်၊ အဖြစ်မြတ်လှ၊ ဗြဟ္မဏဟု၊ တွင်ထမည်သာ၊
အင်္ဂါသုံးမည်၊ ကျေးဇူးတည်လျက်၊ ရွာပြည်တိုင်းကား၊
လှည့်ပတ်သွား၍၊ ထုံးသားမှန်ကူ၊ ခရဖြူနှင့်၊ ပစ္စုဝတ်လဲ၊
လက်ဝဲပတ်ခြို၊ ပစယ်ရှိလျက်၊ တင်တုံစလွယ်၊ လက်ဝယ်မကင်း၊
ခရသင်းနှင့်၊ သလင်းရထည်း၊ ပတ်စည်းကျစ်လစ်၊ ဦးရစ်ပေါင်းထုပ်၊

---

[112] It is a machine in direct translation of the Burmese word စက် (Sak).

[113] A metaphor of perfection. Here, it refers to solid perfection filled with skill and knowledge.

နောက်ထုံးအုပ်လျက်၊ တုန်လှုပ်မဲ့လျှင်း၊ ပွဲလယ်ကျင်း၍၊ စိုးမင်းတို့ရှေ့၊
မရွေ့မတ်မတ်၊ ဘောင်ဘောင်ရွတ်လျက်၊ စိမ်းလတ်မြသွင်၊
နေဇာပင်နှင့်၊ ရေစင်ကမ်းမှတ်၊ ကျင့်မြဲဝတ်ဖြင့်၊ သူမြတ်တို့ထံ၊
အလှူခံလော့။ ခြိုးခြံသိပ်သည်း၊ ဥစ္စာဆည်းလျက်၊ ပစ္စည်းပေါယယ်၊
ဗြဟ္မာကြွယ်ဟု၊ လူဝယ်သတင်းပေါက်စေမင်း။ ။

50.

The one who knows the three books of
Sama, Yajur and Rig Veda;
Who is righteous with good conduct;
Who is a pure descent
From the parents of holy caste;
These are the three features of a Brahmana.
Be faithful to your birth.
When you go about the villages
And cities in the country,
Mark your forehead with the white lime,
Do it before a mirror for perfection.
Your clothes must be white,
Like the white mollusc shell.
Put on your ritual sash
Around your left shoulder,
It must be symmetrical like jasmine petals,
Across the chest down to the waist.
In your hand must be the conch.
The marble white cloth hat,
Wrapped around the head,
Must cover the hair knob at the back.
With no fear,
You must present in the ceremonies,
Before the kings and royals;
Steady and firm,
Powerfully recite the hymns.
Fresh with green Holy Basil,
Sprinkle the sacred water on and about.
With such due devotion to your duty,
You may solicit donations from the nobles.
Live in austerity and save the earnings.
Well to do wealthy Brahmana!
As such, let you be known and talked among the people.

၅၁။^{၁၁၄}

ဥဒည်းမဖျင်၊ နေဝင်အခါ၊ ဆည်းဆာသုံးပါး၊ ပိုင်းခြားဂါထာ၊
ရွတ်မြဲရာသား၊ ကာယာသိဒ္ဓိ၊ တရိသည္ဒာ၊ တတ်လွေ့လာလျက်၊
ကြောင်းခြာခွဲစီ၊ ပရမိသွာ၊ မဟာဗိန္နဲ့၊ ဘေးလွဲ့ရန်ဖီ၊ နတ်စန္ဒီကို၊
ပန်းနီပန်းဖြူ၊ ပူဇော်မူလျက်၊ ဆုယူဆုတောင်း၊ ကျင့်လမ်းဟောင်းဖြင့်၊
ဦးခေါင်းသရွှေး၊ နေ့တိုင်းဆေးရှု၊ လုပ်ကျွေးမှုဆောင်၊
ထဲချောင်တိုက်တွင်း၊ ထမင်းချက်ပြုတ်၊ ငရုတ်ချင်းဆား၊ ဆီပျားသကာ၊
ဃနာထောပတ်၊ ဆုံချွတ်နှမ်းပဲ၊ စားစမြဖြင့်၊ အမဲအဆား၊
သားငါးရှောင်ကြဉ်၊ မဃဥဉ်သက်သတ်၊ ကျင့်မှတ်လွေ့လ၊ စာရိတ္တဖြင့်၊
မိဘစုတော့၊ ခုနှစ်နေ့လျှင်၊ စေ့လတ်သောခါ၊ ကောင်းစွာဆောက်တည်၊
ကိုယ်စားရည်ရှု၊ စိတ်ကြည်မြတ်လေး၊ အလှူပေးလော့၊ ရှေးကလွန်လေ၊
ရှေးရိုးပေသား၊ မျိုးဆွေကျင့်မြဲ၊ မှတ်သုံးစွဲလျက်၊ ငရဲမသက်၊
ခန္ဓာပျက်လည်း၊ အထက်နတ်ပြည် ရောက်စေမင်း။ ။

51.¹¹⁵

At the dawn, the noon and the dusk;
In the three periods,
Regularly recite the assigned hymns.
Strive for the "body perfection."
Master the three sets of recitals,
    in three periods of the day.
Know well when to recite what.
In view of driving away the dangers and evils,
Perform puja to God Parameshwara (Shiva),
    Mahavinayaka (Ganesh), and Chandi Devi.
Worship (them) with the gifts
    of red and white flowers.
Pray for good fortunes.
Preserve the traditions.
Daily perform ritual
    head-washing with fragrance.
Conduct these duties well.
At home, when you prepare food,

---

¹¹⁴ ၁၁၄ See the Appendix-16, p 122, for the explanation of the Pali words and
Vedic terms.
¹¹⁵ See the Appendix-16, p 122, for the explanation of the Pali words and Vedic
terms.

Use the spices, peppers, ginger and salt,
   oil, honey, molasses, milk, butter,
   sesame seeds and legumes;
Cook well and eat well.
Avoid meat, flesh, and fish,
Which are incompatible
    with the vegetarian diet.
Follow the codes of good conduct.
Maintain the good character.
On the passing away of the parents,
On the completion of the day seven,
With good body and mind,
On behalves of the parents, for the parents,
With clear mind and noble thoughts,
Give charities.
These are the rites of the old days,
The traditions coming from the old days,
Ways and manners of the kin and relatives,
Follow and keep them alive.
Thus shall you avoid hell.
When your body perish,
Let you find yourself in heaven.

၅၂။ ၁၁၆

ဂြဟသန္တ၊ ကျမ်းနှင့်ညှိ၍၊ ဗလိပူဇော်၊ ကြိုဟ်ခေါ်ကြိုဟ်နှင်၊
ဗေဒင်ရွတ်မန်း၊ မန္တန်တန်းလျှက်၊ ကျယ်ဝန်းစက္က၊ မဏ္ဍလဟု၊
တစ်ရာ့ရှစ်ကွင်း၊ အင်းလည်းစီရင်၊ ဆင်သားဗိတာန်၊
တမ်းခွန်တစ်လျှောက်၊ ဖြူနီဆောက်၍၊ ပယ်ဖျောက်ရန်ဘော၊
ဆေးပေဦးခေါင်း၊ ဘိသိက်လောင်း၍၊ သူကောင်းသူမြတ်၊
လွတ်စေအနာ၊ ဥဒဒ်ခွါလော့။
ပြည်ရွာတိုင်းကား၊ ကြီးပွားစိမ့်ငှာ၊ လေးမျက်နှာမှ၊
မလာရန်စစ်၊ မဖြစ်စေမှု၊ တိုင်တည်ပြု၍၊ စုသည်ရဲရဲ၊ မီးကျီးခဲ၍၊
မြှောက်ကြံဖြောက်ဖြောက်၊ ပေါက်ပေါက်စသည်၊ ပန်းငါးမည်ဖြင့်၊ ၁၁၇

---

[116] ၁၁၆ See the Appendix-17, p 124, for the glossaries of Pali and Vedic words.

[117] ၁၁၇ ပန်းငါးမည် (Five Flowers) is the poetic expression of the Five Precepts:
(1) no killing, (2) no stealing, (3) no drinking, (4) no adultery (or no sex in
the given context), and (5) no telling lies. Also see Verse 7, p 5.

ဆောက်တည်မပျက်၊ ခုနစ်ရက်လျှင်၊ ခန့်တွက်ပိုင်းခြား၊ မန္တရားတိ၊
ဖန်များစုရွတ်၊ ပျားထောပတ်နှင့်၊ မီးနတ်ကော်ရော်၊ ယဇ်ပူဇော်၍၊
လူ့တော်ရန်စစ် ပျောက်စေမင်း။   ။

52.[118]

In view of Peace of the Planets (Graha Shanti),
Consult the books and perform Bali Puja.
Invite the favorable Planetary Spirits.
Drive away the undesirable Planetary Spirits.
Recite the Vedic stanzas; sing the Mantras.
Create the wide circle Mandala,
        with 108 geometric icons.
Such shall you make the sacred sign.
Let there be a canopy above it.
Decorate it with white and red fabrics.
In order of overcoming
        the dangers and enemies,
Perform the ritual head washing,
Fulfill ceremonial coronation
        of the nobles and royals.
Thus let them be free
        from illness and distress.
The country, the villages, and the provinces,
For the development and prosperity,
Must be protected in the four directions,
So that the enemies cannot approach.
With such objective,
Make a fire with red embers;
Throw in the corns to pop;
Wear the Five Flowers;[119]
Perform the rites,
        steadfast and strong, for seven days.
Select the designated verses of Mantras,
Recite them repeatedly.
Serve food with honey and butter,
        to the God of Fire.
With such sacred puja,
Let the enemies of humankind vanish.

---

[118] See the Appendix-17, p 124, for the glossaries of Pali and Vedic words.
[119] ပန်းငါးမည် (Five Flowers): see the footnote 117.

၅၃॥

ကျေးဇူးပညာ၊ များစွာဂုဏ်အင်၊ ဗေဒင်တတ်သိ၊ ပညာရှိဟု၊ ကဝိပုဏ္ဏား၊
အများသမိုက်၊ သသိ်ကရိုက်ကို၊ မြိုက်မြိုက်လျှာဖျား၊ စက်လားရဟတ်၊
ပတ်ပတ်သွင်သွင်၊ နှုတ်သိ်လွင်နှင့်၊ ပိပြင်မှုတ်မန်း၊ ဖြိုးဖြိုးဖြန်းလျက်၊
ကျယ်ဝန်းထွေပြား၊ အပါးပါးတည်၊ မှတ်သားကိန်းခန်း၊ ဆန်းအလက်ာ၊
နားဝင်စွာ၍၊ ဂါထာဖွဲ့စွမ်း၊ ချီးမွမ်းစလောက်၊ မင်းပွဲမှောက်တွင်၊
တစ်ယောက်ပဏ္ဍိတ်၊ ပုရောဟိတ်ဟု၊ ဘိသိက်ဆရာ၊ မြှောက်ထိုက်စွာသား၊
ဒိသာပါမုက်၊ မည်ထုတ်ကျော်အောင်၊ ကြိုးပမ်းဆောင်လျက်၊
တတ်ခေါင်လိမ္မာ၊ ရှေးအခါ၌၊ ဆရာမောက်လှ၊ ဇာနက္ကသို့၊
လုံ့လကြိုးစား၊ မင်းတို့အားကို၊ စီးပွားရွက်ဆောင်၊
ကျေးဇူးရောင်ဖြင့်၊ လူ့ဘောင်ထွန်လင်း တောက်စေမင်း॥   ॥

53.

Having much knowledge;
Strong with reputation; Skilled in Vedas;
Learned is he; A Master Ponna!
Thus, people must recognize you.
The Sanskrit language
        must be at the tip of your tongue.
Like the revolving pinions of the machine,
Regular and rhythmic,
With sweet and pleasant notes,
You must recite and sing, sweet to the ears.
Far and wide, shower down the mantras.
Wide, broad, diversified, and numerous,
Vedic methods must you know.
With the arts of Vedic investigations,
        presentations, and the recitals,
You must be an expert in the subject.
Must be praise-worthy,
Before the royal audience.
"A Pundit is he," "A Professor is he,"
A Coronation Master,
Qualified and accredited,
A teacher of the world!
As such, you must earn your fame.
Long, long ago,
Most learned and wise,

Teacher of the teachers was Zanakka.[120]
Like him, be industrious and work hard.
Serve the king;
Bring many benefits to him.
With bright colors of loyal service,
Make yourself shine in the human world.

၅၄॥

လက္ခဏာ[123] ကြန်၊[122] တတ်ပွန်လေ့လာ၊ မင်းဖြစ်ရာသား၊
လက်ျာဖဝါး၊ အခြားပြက်ပြက်၊ ခြေလယ်တက်ရှူ၊ လက်လည်းထို့သွင်၊
အရေးမြင်မူ၊ မင်းလျှင်စစ်စစ်၊ ဖြစ်အံ့အမြဲ၊ မချွတ်လွဲဟု၊
ဝမ်းထဲမရှိ၊ လည်ဖြတ်ခံလော့॥
ထုံးစံမှတ်သား၊ နည်းနာများကို၊ ပုဏ္ဏားမျိုးကောင်း၊
ရှစ်ယောက်ပေါင်းတွင်၊ ကဆောင်းတတ်လွန်၊ ကောဏ္ဍည်း[123] ဟန်သို့၊
ဟောညွှန်လက္ခဏာ၊ တတ်လှစွာရှု၊ ပညာကဝေ၊ မြှောက်သောထွေဖြင့်၊
အသေအချာ၊ နည်းနာသိပွ၊ ကိစ္စတတ်ပွန်၊ မန္တန်ပြီးစီး၊
နတ်ကြီးသူရဿတီ၊ ပင့်ချီခေါ်ချ၊ စကားရလျက်၊
ပေါက်ပြကျော့ထိတ်၊ ပုရောဟိတ်ဟု၊ ဘိသိက်ဆရာ မြှောက်စေမင်း॥   ॥

54.

The characteristics of the body construct,
Study and know well.
The features of a king-to-be are,
The right foot is flat,
With a raised mound in the center.
The same will be the hand.
When you see such royal features,
"You shall be the king,"
With surety, say beyond doubt.
Without fear in the stomach,
Must dare to risk your neck.

---

[120] See the Appendix-18, p 128, for more information on Zanakka.

[121] ၁၂၁ လက္ခဏာ fron Pali: লক্ষণ, lakkhaṇa: a sign, mark, characteristic, a prognosticative mark, a quality .

[122] ၁၂၂ ကြန် from Pali: कारेति, kāreti: causes to do, build or construct .

[123] ၁၂၃ ကောဏ္ဍည်း Kondanna. Also see the footnote 124.

Be proficient in the "Conventional Standards,"
The "Methods" and the "Techniques."
Eight famous good Ponnas were there.
Among them, the most excellent,
Skilled and knowledgeable was Kondanna. [124]
Like him,
You must know the characteristics;
Skillful, good, and wise in Vedic craft;
Rich in experience, detailed and thorough
      in the science of theories and techniques;
Proficient in arts, and expert in Mantras.
Great goddess is Saraswatī; [125]
Invite her and converse with her;
Learn the words from her.
Distinguish and stand at the top,
Let you be *the* professor,
Accredited with the qualifications of a Coronation Master.

---

[124] According to the Buddhist biographers, King Suddhodana summoned eight most learned astrologers to see his new born son, Siddhartha. Seven of them predicted that Siddhartha would be either a chakravartin (Conqueror of the World) or a Buddha. The youngest astrologer named Kondanna uniquely said that the boy would be Buddha nothing but Buddha. Siddhartha became Buddha. As such, Kondanna is considered the best and the most learned.

[125] *Sarasvatī* सरस्वती Saraswatī, Goddess of Wisdom. See for example , http://en.wikipedia.org/wiki/Saraswati

၅၅ ॥

ကျယ်ဝန်းစကြဝဠာ၊ ကမ္ဘာအစ၊ ပေါ်ဦးကလျှင်၊ ဗြဟ္မာ့နွယ်ရိုး၊
ကျော်ဟိုးဟိုးလျှင်၊ ကောင်းကျိုးစင်ကြယ်၊ လေးသွယ်ဗေဒင်၊
တတ်သိမြင်သား၊ လူတွင်ထင်ရှား၊ ပုဏ္ဏားတို့ကို၊ ကျင့်စေလိုရှ၍၊
သံချိုလက်၊ ထုံးပမာဖြင့်၊ နည်းနာထွေပြား၊ မှတ်စိမ့်ကြားသည်၊
တခြား တတိယပိုင်းတည်း॥ ॥

55.

In this broad and wide universe,
From the beginning of the world,
Since the primordial time,
The Caste of Brahmin is famous and known.
Serene and beneficial,
With the knowledge of four Vedas,
Outstanding among human;
To all Ponna, wishing success,
In these sweet and poetic verses,
Setting the examples, illustrating the parables,
I tell you to learn
Varieties of theories and techniques.
Thus, I end the Third Part.

The End

Translated and explained by Shwe Lu Maung

2.
Popular Stanzas

The verses of Part-1 *Advice to the four kinds of people* are the most popular and known among the people at large. However, the verses from Part-2 *Advice to the king* and Part-3 *Advice to the Ponna* are only known among the academics and scholars because these verses are filled with the Pali vocabularies and heavy to read.

The Romanized versions (transliterations) given here are in the Bama pronunciation since it is widely used in all Myanmar. The stanza by stanza English translations given here may be different from the text of the complete verses, due to the isolation from the full context. The transliteration is a tricky and difficult job. I have used St. John's *Burmese self-taught (in Burmese and Roman characters) with phonetic pronunciation, at https://archive.org/details/burmeseselftaugh00stjorich,* as the standard reference in my transliteration. Every transliterated stanza is subjected to five text to speech software, which are:

1. Text to Voice converter 4.0 by Imaginative World downloaded from http://www.softpedia.com in January 2015. Adult Male # 1 American English was used for speech.
2. http://text-to-speech.imtranslator.net/, used online.
3. http://www.oddcast.com/home/demos/tts/tts_example.php, used online.
4. https://www.ivona.com/, used online, and
5. http://www.ispeech.org/text.to.speech, used online

Among these software, ivona-English American Salli is good at pronouncing the words beginning with the 'hl', 'ht', 'hm', and 'hw' sounds.

The software were used in the months of August, September, and October 2015. Different vowels and consonants of similar sounds were tested with the "text-to-speech" software and *the transliterations which gave the best approximation to the Myanmar sound by the software are selected.* The 'text-to-speech' software cannot pronounce certain Myanmar sounds, in particular, 'ht' (ထ) and 'my' (မျ). Please keep in mind that 'ht' (ထ) is pronounced like in '*Th*ailand' and 'my' (မျ) is pronounced like in '*My*anmar.' Nevertheless, the reader is advised to consult a Myanmar speaker to get perfection.

1. These two stanzas are popular for their opening message.

Popular stanzas from Verse 1; Stanza Number: see under the S.no.			
S. no.	Myanmar	transliteration	English
1	ကြားပိမ့်သူမြတ်	jyar bint Thu Mrat	Thu Mrat shall speak;
2	အများမှတ်စိမ့်။	A myar hmat sint	so, people may learn.

(Thu Mrat is the name of a Rakhine person. Therefore, it is pronounced in the Rakhine sound).

2. Verse 2 is the most popular for its bearing of the highest ethical standard. It is taught at schools. Almost everyone knows the last three stanzas, that is the stanza 12, 13 and 14.

Popular stanzas from Verse 2; Stanza Number: see under the S.no.			
S. no.	Myanmar	transliteration	English
12	ကောင်းမှုမြတ်နိုး	kaung hmu, myat noe	Love to be good
13	ကောင်းအောင်ကြိုးရှု	kaung aung, kjo ywayt	strive to be good, and
14	ကောင်းကျိုး ကိုယ့်၌ တည်စေမင်း။ ။	kaung kjo, ko hnight, tae sey min	Institute in you good.

3. These stanzas are popular for their reflection of basic Buddhist ethics.

Popular stanzas from Verse 4; Stanza Number: see under the S.no.			
S. no.	Myanmar	transliteration	English
1	ဆန္ဒဒေါသာ	Hsann-dha, daut thaar	The desire, the anger,
2	ဘယာမောဟ	Bha yar, mau hah	the fear, the delusion
3	အပါယ်ကျသား	apay jhya thaar	lead to hell.

4. These stanzas are popular for its contrasting good from evil.

Popular stanzas from Verse 6; Stanza Number: see under the S.no.

S. no.	Myanmar	transliteration	English
1	ပညာမျက်စိ	piññya myak si	The eyes of wisdom,
2	မြင်မရှိ၍	myin mashi ywayt	Lacking; therefore,
3	မသိတရား	mathi ta-yar	Does not know the truth,
4	အယူမှားလျက်	ayu hmãr layet	the wrong prevails
5	စီးပွားမမြော်	sii puor ma-myaw	No prosperity in sight
6	ကျိုးမပေါ်သား	kjo mapaw thar	No benefit comes
7	သူတော်မဟုတ်	thutaw mahote	Not a good person
8	ယုတ်သည်စရိုက်	yoat thi syite	With a wicked character
9	လူသူမိုက်ကို	lu thu mite ko	A man of darkness
10	မကြိုက်မချစ်	Ma hjite ma chit	Don't like or love him
11	ရန်သူစစ်သို့	Yan thu siit thoh	Consider him an enemy
12	မနှစ်သက်ပဲ	Ma hnit thet pày	With disapproval
13	ဝေးစွာရဲ၍	Way swar shày ywayt	Stay away from him
14	အမြဲခွာရှင်း ဖဲကြဉ်မင်း။ ။	Amyey kwar shinn phày kji min	Always, keep a distance; avoid him from afar.

5. Verse 7 is very popular for its teaching of tolerance and five principles of ethic. It is taught at school and the students have to recite it by heart.

S. no.	Myanmar	transliteration	English
	Popular stanzas from Verse 7; Stanza Number: see under the S.no.		
1	ပါဏာတိပါတ်	par na tit pat,	No killing
2	မသတ်သူ့သက်	ma thet, thuu thek,	
3	ခိုးဝှက်မမူ	kho whak, ma mu,	No stealing
4	မယူသေစာ	mayu, thay sar,	No drinking
5	အိမ်ရာမမှား	in yar, ma-hmar,	No adultery
6	မုသားမဆို	muuthar, mahso,	No telling lies
7	ကိုယ်ကိုနှိမ့်ချ	kooko, nhit cha,	Be humble
8	စောင့်သီလနှင့်	saunt thila, ñit,	maintain the Sila
9	ဒါနလှူဝတ်	darna, hlue waat,	Charity
10	ရက်မချွတ်လျှင်	yaek machuat, lahyin,	Give every day
11	မပြတ်ဆောက်တည်	mapyat, hsauk tee,	Always strive
12	ဆုကြီးရည်၍	hsu jee, yee ywayt,	with the goal of Great Trophy
13	မကြည်ခိုက်ရန်	ma je, khite yan,	animosity and quarrel
14	သူကျူးလွန်လည်း	thu, q lwan lee	Even if someone commits
15	မျက်မာန်မပြင်း သိမ်းလေမင်း॥ ॥	myak man, ma p-yin, thing lay min.	Control the anger and Respond with restraint.

Translated and explained by Shwe Lu Maung

6. These stanzas are popular for their reflection of the parents' place in the society.

Popular stanzas from Verse 8; Stanza Number: see under the S.no.			
S. no.	Myanmar	transliteration	English
1	မိခင်ဖခင်	Me khin phaa kin	The mother, the father
2	ကျေးဇူးရှင်ကို	kjey zoo shin ko	are the Benefactors
3	ချစ်ခင်မြတ်နိုး	chit khin myăt no	Love and respect them fondly
4	ရုပုထိုးသို့	gu pa htoe thŏ	Like a pagoda.

7. These stanzas are popular for their ethical values.

Popular stanzas from Verse 11; Stanza Number: see under the S.no.			
S. no.	Myanmar	transliteration	English
1	လောဘ ဒေါသ	laubha dautha	Greed, anger, (and)
2	မောဟသူပျက်	mawha thu pyaek	delusion are the evils.
11	စိတ်ဆင်ရိုင်း [ ]	sait hsin yine [ ]	the mind is the 'Wild Elephant'

8. These stanzas are popular for teaching to learn when young.

Popular stanzas from Verse 13; Stanza Number: see under the S.no.			
S. no.	Myanmar	transliteration	English
1	ထုံးတီးနည်းနာ	htoon tee nee na	arts, science, technology
2	အဖြာဖြာ၌	a phyăr phyăr hnight	of many disciplines
3	ပညာရှာမှီး	piññya shar hmie	search, learn knowledge

4	မကြီးသက်ရွယ်	magyi thek ywey	before the old age
5	အငယ်သော်က	a-ngay thaw gha	when being young
6	ကြိုးလုံ့လလျက်	kjoo loon lah layet	put great effort

9. Verse 15 is popular for its emphasis of learning a profession or specialization of a subject.

Popular stanzas from Verse 15; Stanza Number: see under the S.no.		
S. no.	Myanmar	transliteration	English
1	သူတော်တကာ	thu taw tagah	Everyone
2	တတ်စရာသား	tet sa yah thar	has to learn
3	အဋ္ဌာရသ	Ahtar ra thah	Varieties of subjects and knowledge
4	သိပ္ပံအပြား	thik-pa a p-yar	
5	အတတ်များကို	atet myah ko	(and) technologies
6	မှတ်သားသတိ	Hmat thar tha ti	to note in the mind
7	ပညာရှိတို့	piññya shi tŏ	the learned people
8	တတ်သိအပ်စွ॥	Tet thi et saub	must learn and know.
9	ထိုသိပ္ပံကို	hto thik-pa ko	all the subjects
10	နှံ့မျှလုံးခြို	Hnãh hmyă loon choon	all the disciplines
11	မတတ်တုံလည်း	ma tet toan laey	though difficult to know
12	တစ်စုံတစ်ခု	ta saon ta khuu	One or any subject
13	တတ်အောင်ပြု၍	tet aung pyuu ywayt	make sure to learn and specialize
14	လူမှုအိမ်ထောင်	Lu hmu iin htaung	(so that) to family and society
15	စီးပွားဆောင်လော့॥	si puor saung laut	(you) will bring the prosperity.
16	ညဉ့်မှောင်မသိ	Nya hmaung ma thi	Does not know the darkness of the night

17	ကြက်မျက်စိသို့	Kjek myet si thŏ	Like the chicken eyes
18	မိမိကိုယ်ဖို့	Me mi koh phŏ	In yourself
19	အတတ်ချို့သော်	A tet chŏ thaw	If knowledge lacks
20	သူတို့ပြစ်တင်	Thu tŏ pyit tin	People will scorn you
21	ဆင်းရဲဖျင်အံ့။	Sinn yè phyin añt	And you will suffer
22	ထင်ထင်မျက်မြော်	Htin htin myek myaw	look clearly to the future
23	မကော်ရော်သည်	Ma kaw yaw thi	Do not invite disrespect
24	အိုသော် လူမရယ် စေနှင့်မင်း။	O'thaw lu mayey sae ñit min	In your old age, don't be a subject to laughed at.

10. Verse 16 is popular for its reflection of the complexity of a family life. The Verse sends many men and women into the monastic life.

Popular stanzas from Verse 16; Stanza Number: see under the S.no.			
S. no.	Myanmar	transliteration	English
1	ဃရာဝါသ	Garar wah tha	A clan-household
2	သမ္ဗာဓဟု	Thambada huu	Is a corporation
3	ကိစ္စမြားမြောင်	Kissa myar myaung	There are endless matters
4	လူတို့ဘောင်၌	Lu doe phaung hnight	In this human society
5	အိမ်ထောင်သက်မွေး	Inn htaung thek mweey	Having a family and livelihood
6	ခြနှယ်မြွေးသား	Cha nay myēy thar	Complex like a web of the termites
7	လူရေးကျယ်စွာ	Lu yey kjay swar	Human affairs are wide, broad,
8	အဖြာဖြာကို	a phyăr phyăr ko	(and) numerous
9	လိမ္မာအတတ်	Lane mar a tet	Be wise and skillful

10	ချားရဟတ်သို့.	Charr ya hat thǒ	like a windmill
11	လှည့်ပတ်ပြီးမှ	Hlát pat p-yi hmǎ	go all around
12	ကြံတွက်ဆလျက်	Kjan twut hsa layet	Think and plan well
13	လုံ့လပင်စည်	Lǒn la pin si	Strong effort
14	အရင်းတည်က	A-yin tee ka	If you invest
15	ခက်ရှည်ပညာ	Khet shey piññya	(and) Lengthen your wisdom
16	ချမ်းသာအသီး	Chan thaar a-thi	The fruit of wealth
17	ကြီးစရွေ့.ရွေ့.	kjee sa ywayt ywayt	Will start growing
18	အဒလေ့ဖြင့်	A-da leyt fient	Live a disciplined life
19	မမေ့မကျန်	Ma mae ma kjan	Do not forget or neglect
20	လူမှုပွန်လျက်	Loo hmu pawñ layet	Fulfil the social duties
21	စောင်မာန်မဲ့ဆုံး	Saung man mǎe sone	Have no pride or prejudice
22	တော်ဖြောင့်သုံးရွှ	Taw fyont thoon ywayt	Be knowledgeable and honest
23	နှလုံးသန့်.စင် ကြယ်စေမင်း။ ။	Hnǎ loon thant sinh kjay sae min	Let your heart be clean and shine like a star

11. These stanzas are popular for placing the mother higher than Mt. Meru, the most important and highest place of the cosmos.

Popular stanzas from Verse 17; Stanza Number: see under the S.no.		
S. no.	Myanmar	transliteration	English
1	လေးကျွန်းထိပ်ခေါင်	Lay jywan htit khong	The peak of the four Islands
2	မြင်းမိုရဲ့တောင်နှင့်	Myint Moh taung ñit	With, Mt. Meru

3	ချိန်ဆောင်နှိုင်းလည်း	Chain taung hnigh lee	Even when compared
4	အတိုင်းမသိ	Atai ma thi	Immeasurable
5	ကျေးဇူးရှိသည်	Kjay zoo shi thi	Gratitude indebted to
6	အမိကားတိုက်	Ami gah tite	the mother is the world

12. Verse 18 is popular for its teaching of how to save and be wealthy. It is taught at school and the students have to recite it by heart.

Popular stanzas from Verse 18; Stanza Number: see under the S.no.

S. no.	Myanmar	transliteration	English
1	စေ့မြေ့သိပ်သည်း	Saet myeat thait thï	Be meticulous
2	ရွှေ့ရွှေ့ဆည်းသော်	ywayt ywayt hsee laut	make regular saving
3	စရည်းအိုးခွက်	Sa yi o'kwaet	Lacquered earthen pot
4	ကြီးစွာလျက်လျှင်	Kji swar layet lee	no matter how big
5	တံစက်ကျများ	Tan saht kja myar	Drop by drop
6	ပြည့်သောလားသို့	P-yi thaw laar thö	can be filled up
7	ပျား၏နည်းထုံး	Pia ee nee htone	The way of the bees
8	မှတ်ကျင့်သုံးရှု	Hmat kjint thone ywayt	Follow and act, and
9	ခြခုံးတောင်ပို့	Chã pone taung pö	the ant mounds
10	ဖို့သည့်ခြင်းရာ	Phö thë chin ya	see how the ants make
11	လူလိမ္မာတို့	Lu lain mar tö	Likewise, O'wise people
12	ဥစ္စာဆည်းထွေ	Oat sah hsii htway	Build wealth
13	တတ်လှုစေလော့။	Suu tet sae laut	Learn to save
14	ကြွက်သေတစ်ခု	Kjwat thay ta khu	With a dead rat

15	အရင်းပြု၍	A-yin p-yu ywayt	as the capital
16	ကြွယ်မှုတတ်ဆုံး	Kjway wa tet hsone	(he) became the wealthiest
17	သူဌေးထုံးကို	Thu htay htone ko	This rich man's path
18	နှလုံးမူလျက်၊	Hna loon mu layet	Keep in your heart
19	ကြံစည်နက်၍	Kjan se net ywayt	Think deep and plan
20	သူထက်လွန်ကဲ ကြွယ်စေမင်း။ ။	Thu htet lwun kè kjway sae min	be richest of the rich.

13. These stanzas are popular for their figurative and poetic beauty.

Popular stanzas from Verse 19; Stanza Number: see under the S.no.			
S. no.	Myanmar	transliteration	English
1	လုံ့လပညာ	Lŏn la piññya	Be industrious and educated
2	လိမ္မာတတ်ကုံ	lain mar tet kon	be wise and skilled,
3	ဆင်စွယ်စုံသို့	Hsin sway sone thŏ	Like a tusker elephant,
27	ကျင့်နည်းညံ့ဆုံး	Kjint htone ñyant sone	Most inferior ways
28	သူပျက်ထုံးကို	Thu p-yet htone ko	(of) the characterless people.
29	နှလုံးမငြိ တွယ်စေနှင့်မင်း။ ။	Hna loon ma gnyi twey sae ñit min	Don't let your heart entangle there.

14. Verse 20 is popular verses for its teaching to be a benefactor to the relatives, friends and people at large like a gigantic banyan tree that gives shade, shelter and food to the travellers and birds. It is a beautiful poem with lovely metaphors. It is taught at school and the students have to recite by heart.

Popular stanzas from Verse 20; Stanza Number: see under the S.no.

S. no.	Myanmar	transliteration	English
1	ကျောင်းတော်ခရီး	Kjaung taw kha yee	On the journey to the Temple
2	လမ်းမကြီး၌	Lan ma jee hnight	on the highway
3	ပင်ထီးပညောင်	Pin htee pa nyaung	A huge Banyan tree
4	မြစ်တစ်ထောင်နှင့်	Myit ta htung ñit	with one thousand roots
5	မြှားမြှောင် ခက်လက်	Myar myaung khet let	Numerous branches and sub-branches
6	ရွက်လည်းစိပ်စိပ်	Ywat lee sik sik	Covered with thick leaves
7	စေ့စေ့သိပ်လျက်၊	Sè sè thick layet	layers after layers
8	ရိပ်လည်းမြိုင်မြိုင်	Yeik lee myaing myaing	The shade is cool
9	လေမနိုင်လျှင်	Lay ma nai la-yin	the wind cannot win the tree
10	ပွတ်နိုင်သီးမှည့်	Pyaw-ut khine thi hmiet	Filled with the ripe fruits
11	အပြည့်ကျေးငှက်	A pêi kjey ngat	Full of birds
12	စားလျက် သောင်းသဲ	Sah layet thaung thaey	Eating and singing
13	မှီဝဲလူဗိုလ်	Hmi waì boh lu	People and soldiers under its shade
14	ရိပ်ခို အများ	Yeit kho a-myar	Taking shelter
15	ခရီးသွားတို့	Khayi tha-uw doè	The wayfarers
16	နေနားပျော်ရွှင်	Nay nah p-yau she-win	Rest, relax and enjoy

Translated and explained by Shwe Lu Maung

17	ထိုသစ်ပင်ကား	Hto thit pin gah	That tree
18	ဝင်လာသသူ	Win la tha thu	Whoever comes under it
19	ခပ်သိမ်းလူကို	Khet thing lu ko	One and all
20	ဆာပူငြိမ်းအောင်	Hsaar puh ñ-ying aung	Gives relief from the burning heat
21	စီးပွားဆောင်သို့	Si puor hsaung thoĕ	beneficent as such
22	လူ့ဘောင် ကောင်းကြွယ်	Lŭ baung kaung kjoay	for the benefit of the society
23	လူကိုကယ်လည်း	Lu gon k lee	a person of wealth and strength
24	ထိုနှယ် လည်းကောင်း	Hto nae lee kaung	Likewise, in that way
25	ဖြစ်တုံ့ရှောင်ရှ	hpiit toan shaung ywayt	Must act
26	မျိုးပေါင်းဆွေဝါး	Myo bhaung swey wor	To the relatives and kin
27	လူအများကို	Lu a myar ko	To the people at large
28	သနားကြင်နာ	Tha-nar kjin nar	With sympathy and kindness
29	စီးပွားရှာရှ	Si puor shar ywayt	With the wealth you have
30	မေတ္တာမကင်	Me-yeat ta ma kinn	With love
31	မစခြင်းဖြင့်	Mah sa chin pha-yint	With helping mind
32	ထံရင်းမှီကိုးကွယ် စေမင်း॥ ॥	Htan yiin hme, ko kway sae min	Make yourself a host and shelter

15. Verse 21 is among the most popular verses for the teaching of social conduct. It is taught at school and the students have to recite by heart.

S. no.	Myanmar	transliteration	English
Popular stanzas from Verse 21; Stanza Number: see under the S.no.			
1	ျပူျပူႏွာႏွာ	P-u p-u hgnāh hgnāh	Be friendly and welcoming
2	လူတကာကို	Lu ta-gah ko	to everybody
3	သာသာခ်ိဳခ်ိဳ	Thaa thaa cho cho	Sweet and gentle
4	ခ်စ္ဖြယ္ဆိုရွ႕	Chit fo-way soh ywayt	speak lovely
5	စိုစိုျပည္ျပည္	So so piay piay	Bright and cheerful
6	ခ်စ္မႈနည္းႏွင့္	Chit mu nae ñit	nurture lovely manners
7	လည္လည္ပတ္ပတ္	Lay lay pêt pêt	Be knowledgeable and understanding
8	ေလာကဝတ္၌	Lauka wet hnight	In the societal ways and manners
9	ျပတ္ျပတ္သားသား	P-yat p-yat thaar thaar	Be clear and precise
10	အျပားျပားလ်ွင္	A p-yar p-yar lahyin	in all matters
11	မႈမ်ားခပ္သိမ္း	hmu myar khat thing	every case
12	ေဆာင္တိုင္းၿငိမ္းလ်က္	Hsaung tai ñien layet	Make peaceful ending
13	သူစိမ္းသူက်က္	Thu sainn thu kjet	Stranger or friend
14	ေပါင္းဖက္သေရြ႕	Paung phet tha ywayt	when you meet
15	မိဘေတြ႕သို႔	Mi pha twaet thŏ	as though you meet your parents
16	ေမြ႕ေမြ႕ေလ်ာ္ေလ်ာ္	Maway maway lah-yaw lah-yaw	Make it feel good

17	ပျော်ပျော်ပါးပါး	P-yaw p-yaw pāh pāh	Happy with light heart
18	နှုတ်ချိုပျားနှင့်	Hnoat cho pyah ñit	lips sweet like honey
19	ဝတ်စားပေးပွဲ	Wãt saa pay pant	Provide clothing, food, and shelter
20	ဖြည့်ဖြူးနဲ့လျက်	Phie few hnant layet	Distribute to everyone
21	အလွှဲ့ကျွန်ကျေး	A lwant kjan kyay	Slaves and servants
22	ဆွေသားမြေးကို	Sway thar miey ko	friends, relatives, children, and grandchildren
23	ကျေးမွေး မည့ိုးငယ်စေမင်း॥ ॥	Kjway hmway ma hnyo ngay sae min	Treat them well; do not let them feel small or neglected.

16. These stanzas are popular for teaching to the king to follow the ten codes of King's conduct.

Popular stanzas from Verse 23; Stanza Number: see under the S.no.		
S. no.	Myanmar	transliteration	English
22	ဆယ်ထွေစောင့်ကြပ်	Say htwey saunt kjat	Uphold the ten laws
23	တရားကွပ်၍	Ta ya kwyat ywayt	Maintain the precepts

17. These stanzas are popular for teaching how to earn the love of human and heavenly being, and the way of life living with civility.

Popular stanzas from Verse 24; Stanza Number: see under the S.no.		
S. no.	Myanmar	transliteration	English
21	လူနတ်ချစ်ဖွယ်	Lu nat chit pha-way	Be lovely to the human and heavenly beings

| 22 | ကျေးဇူးကြွယ်လျက် | Kjay zu kjoey layet | Be beneficent |
| 23 | ကျင့်နှယ်လမ်းရိုး မှန်စေမင်း॥ ॥ | kja-int na-way lan yoe hman sae min | Follow the straight and right path |

18. These stanzas are very popular and freely recited when we talk about the country and national affairs.

Popular stanzas from Verse 26; Stanza Number: see under the S.no.			
S. no.	Myanmar	transliteration	English
1	ပြည်တဲ့အရေး	P-yi htey a-yeh	The country affairs are
2	ပေါက်နှင့်ကျေးသို့	Pauk ñit kjey thŏ	like "Pauk and Kyey."
3	ကြံတွေးလှ့ည်ကာ	Kjan twey hlayt gah	think of which is which
4	မသိသာတည့်॥	Ma thi thar dae-it	(it is) hard to know

19. These stanzas are popular for the advice how to be a good and lovely friend.

Popular stanzas from Verse 27; Stanza Number: see under the S.no.			
S. no.	Myanmar	transliteration	English
20	မိတ်မှန်းကိုယ်ကို	Maite hmam koh ko	Be a good friend
21	တဲ့တစ်ဆိုရ့ဲ	Tan tit hso ywayt	With assurance
22	ချစ်လိုစကား မှန်စေမင်း॥ ॥	Chit lo sagar hman sae min	Be true to your lovely words

20. These stanzas are popular for the reflection of the basic Buddhist teaching.

Popular stanzas from Verse 28; Stanza Number: see under the S.no.			
S. no.	Myanmar	transliteration	English
16	သုံးပေါ်မြတ်စွာ	Thon phaw myat swah	Three Holly Ones
17	ရတနာကို	Ya-ta nah ko	Are the jewels
18	မကွာကပ်ဆည်း	Ma kwah kat hsee	Worship always

21. These stanzas are popular for the classic expression of peace and serenity of the moon.

Popular stanzas from Verse 29; Stanza Number: see under the S.no.			
S. no.	Myanmar	transliteration	English
15	အရောင်ချမ်းလွန်	A yaung chan la-on	Lovely and serene
16	လဗိမာန်လျှင်	La bie mañ lahyin	The heavenly Moon
17	ပူပန်မရှိ	Pu pan mashi	makes worry-free
18	ငြိမ်းစေဘိရှ့	Nyein sae bhi thŏ	and peaceful;

22. These stanzas are popular for advising the king to love his soldiers as his own sons.

Popular stanzas from Verse 30; Stanza Number: see under the S.no.			
S. no.	Myanmar	transliteration	English
25	ချစ်ကြိုက်သနား	Chit kjite tha nar	Love and care (them)
26	ရင်ခွဲ့သားသို့	Yin hnight thaar thŏ	like your own sons
27	ဖြည့်ဖြားမင်းရေး ပွန်စေမင်း‖ ‖	Ph-yit phyaah min yé p-won sae min	Be skillful in your delivery of kingship.

23. These stanzas are popular for their poetic beauty of advice given to the king.

Popular stanzas from Verse 31; Stanza Number: see under the S.no.		
S. no.	Myanmar	transliteration	English
28	ပြည်သူ့မျက်ပွင့်	P-yi thu myak p-wint	O'pupil of the people's eyes,
29	ကောင်းအောင်ကျင့်လေ့။	Kaung aung kjint laut	Strive to be good and act well.

24. These stanzas are popular for their poetic beauty in the expression of the overcoming hardship and depression.

Popular stanzas from Verse 33; Stanza Number: see under the S.no.		
S. no.	Myanmar	transliteration	English
37	တိမ်တိုက်လှစ်ထွန်း	Tin tite hlit htun	shines through the thick cloud
38	လအဝန်းသို့	La awunn thŏ	like the moon

25. These stanzas are popular for the poetic expression of the mythical flower which is considered the most beautiful and the sweetest.

Popular stanzas from Verse 34; Stanza Number: see under the S.no.		
S. no.	Myanmar	transliteration	English
25	ရတနာမြဂူ	Ya-ta nah mya gu	the Cave of Jade
26	နန္ဒမုန့်	Nandamu hnight	in the "Happiness,"
27	မဉ္ဇူပန်းလား	Myitzu paan laar	Like the Myitzu Flower
28	ကျော်ထင်ရှားလျက်	Kjaw htin shaar layet	Let it bloom to the fame.

Translated and explained by Shwe Lu Maung

26. These stanzas are popular for the advice how to fight with a lightening speed.

Popular stanzas from Verse 35; Stanza Number: see under the S.no.		
S. no.	Myanmar	transliteration	English
42	ရွပ်ရွပ်ထိုးခုတ်	Ywat ywat htoe khoat	Fight with the lightening speed
43	ကြက်ရဲစုတ်သို့	Kjat yey soat thŏ	Like the kite swoops down on the chicken

27. These stanzas are popular for the advice to be brave and ferocious like a lion.

Popular stanzas from Verse 36; Stanza Number: see under the S.no.		
S. no.	Myanmar	transliteration	English
37	ကြမ်းခက်ရဲမာန်	Kjann khet yey maan	Ferocious and brave
38	ခြေသေ့ဟန်သို့	Chin thae han thŏ	Like a lion

28. These stanzas are popular for advising to keep water and food sufficient for all.

Popular stanzas from Verse 37; Stanza Number: see under the S.no.		
S. no.	Myanmar	transliteration	English
14	ပြည်ကြီးလက္ခဏာ	P-yi kji letkhanar	The feature of a great country
15	ရေစာလောက်ငံ့	Yay sah lout ngant	Water and food must be sufficient for all.

29. These stanzas are popular for the depiction of a king's place and responsibility.

Popular stanzas from Verse 38; Stanza Number: see under the S.no.

S. no.	Myanmar	transliteration	English
1	အခေါင်ကြုၩန်း	A khaung kja ñgaan	Crown of the throne
2	လူ့ထိပ်ထွန်းသား	Luu htick htun thaar	Supreme of the people
3	ဦးစွန်းအချာ	Oo chaun a char	The vertex and pinnacle
4	မင်းတကာတို့	Min ta-gah dŏ	Are the kings

30. These stanzas are popular for the advice for having disciplines and codes of conduct in every matter.

Popular stanzas from Verse 39; Stanza Number: see under the S.no.

S. no.	Myanmar	transliteration	English
28	ဟူဟူသရွေ့	whu whu tha ywayt	In all matters
29	အဓလေ့ဖြင့်	A dha layt fient	Establish a code of conduct

31. These stanzas are popular for the poetic metaphors of knowledge and evils.

Popular stanzas from Verse 40; Stanza Number: see under the S.no.

S. no.	Myanmar	transliteration	English
20	မျက်ရှင်အလား	Myat shin a laar	Like the Third Eye
21	ပညာအားလျှင်	Piññya ār lahyin	Is the Prowess of Knowledge
45	သူပျက်သုံးယောက်	Thu p-yat thon youk	the Three Bad Entities
46	ပါယ်မကြောက်ကို	Péy ma kjauk ko	That are unafraid of hell.

32. These stanzas are very popular for their philosophical expression of the endlessness. Here, they are used to depict the vastness of the ocean. Commonly, they are used to highlight the endlessness of 'Saṃsāra' or 'the cycle of birth and rebirth.'

S. no.	Myanmar	transliteration	English
1	အပ္ပမေယျ	eppa may ya	Immeasurable
2	အနန္တ လျှင်	Ananda lahyin	Endless and
3	ဆုံးစမထင်	Soon sa ma htin	infinite
4	ကမ်းမမြင်သား	Kam ma myin thaar	No land in sight

Popular stanzas from Verse 41; Stanza Number: see under the S.no.

33. These stanzas are popular for their plain expression of righteousness and justice.

S. no.	Myanmar	transliteration	English
25	အကြားတည့်မှန်	Ajar tè hman	Unswayed, right in the middle,
26	ချိန်ခွင်ဟန်သို့	Chayn khuin han thŏ	Like a balance
27	ဧကန်ကျကျ	Ay kan kjâ kjâ	with one mind

Popular stanzas from Verse 42; Stanza Number: see under the S.no.

34. These stanzas are popular for their simple expression of temporariness.

S. no.	Myanmar	transliteration	English
32	ဖေါက်လဲတတ်စွာ	Faut lè tat swah	Impermanent is
33	သက်ခန္ဓာကား	Thet khanhtar gah	this life and body;
34	အခါမြင့်ရှည်	A khah myint shēy	For a long time,
35	မတည်နိုင်ဘူး။	Ma tee naing boo	It does not last.

Popular stanzas from Verse 44; Stanza Number: see under the S.no.

35. These stanzas are popular for their common expression of judgment.

Popular stanzas from Verse 45; Stanza Number: see under the S.no.		
S. no.	Myanmar	transliteration	English
38 အပြစ်ပေးကောင်း	A p-yit pāy gaung	Punish or
39 မပေးကောင်းဟု	Ma pāy gaung huu	Not to punish

36. These stanzas are popular for highlighting the benefit of having anger controlled.

Popular stanzas from Verse 46; Stanza Number: see under the S.no.		
S. no.	Myanmar	transliteration	English
45	ပညာတိုင်းတည်း	Piññya tine tee	With due wisdom,
46	မျက်မာန်နည်းမှု	Myak man nee mu	When anger is kept lowest,
47	လူလည်းပြောဟော	Lu lee p-yaw haw	People will talk good of it;
48	နတ်ချစ်မောသည်	Nat chit maw thi	Heaven will love you for it.
49	ကျော်စောကောင်းချီး ၌ဝေမင်း။ ॥	Kjaw swoah kaung chee ñgar sae min	Therefore, your fame of goodness will travel far and wide.

37. These stanzas are popular for the common expression of a physician's knowledge and fame.

Popular stanzas from Verse 48; Stanza Number: see under the S.no.		
S. no.	Myanmar	transliteration	English
42	ကိုးဆယ့်ခြောက်ပါး	coh sait chaut paar	The ninety-six kinds of illness,

43	အပြားပြားကို	A p-ya p-ya ko	In all varieties,
44	မမှားလွတ်အောင်	Ma hmah lwut aung	no mistake, no miss
45	ကုသဆောင်၍	Kuu tha saung ywayt	treat well
46	အခေါင်သမား မြောက်စေမင်း။ ။	A khaung thamar myaut sae min	Make yourself the greatest medicine man.

38. These stanzas are popular for the common expression of an astrologer's knowledge.

Popular stanzas from Verse 49; Stanza Number: see under the S.no.			
S. no.	Myanmar	transliteration	English
25	ဂြိုဟ်နင်းဂြိုဟ်ပြောင်း	Joe nin joe p-yong	The planetary position and transition
26	ကောင်းမကောင်းသား	Kaung ma kaung tha	Is it good or bad?
27	ကျိုးကြောင်းဆုံးဖြတ်	Kjo kjaung soon fy-yat	You must be able to tell.

39. These stanzas are popular for the depiction of a Ponna (Brahmana) in the ceremonies and pujas.

Popular stanzas from Verse 50; Stanza Number: see under the S.no.			
S. no.	Myanmar	transliteration	English
29	မရွေ့မတ်မတ်	Ma ywayt pat pat	Steady and firm
30	ဘောင်ဘောင်ရွတ်လျက်	Baung baung ywat layet	Powerfully recite the hymns.

40. These stanzas are popular for the illustration of the red and white flowers commonly used in worshiping.

Popular stanzas from Verse 51; Stanza Number: see under the S.no.			
S. no.	Myanmar	transliteration	English
14	ပန်းနီပန်းဖြူ ||	Pann nee pann feu	red and white flowers
15	ပူဇော်မှုလျက်	Pu zaw mu layet	Worship with the gifts

41. These stanzas are popular for the metaphor of the five Buddhist basic precepts.

Popular stanzas from Verse 52; Stanza Number: see under the S.no.			
S. no.	Myanmar	transliteration	English
30	ပန်းငါးမည်ဖြင့်	Pann ngaah myin fient	Wear the Five Flowers
31	ဆောက်တည်မပျက်	Hsaut tee ma p-yet	steadfast and strong

42. These stanzas are popular for teaching how to beautifully recite the mantra.

Popular stanzas from Verse 53; Stanza Number: see under the S.no.			
S. no.	Myanmar	transliteration	English
10	ပတ်ပတ်သွင်သွင်	Pat pat thwin thwin	regular and rhythmic
11	နှတ်သဲလွင်နှင့်	hnoat than lwin ñit	With sweet and pleasant notes

43. These stanzas are popular for depicting the greatness of Saraswatī.

Popular stanzas from Verse 54; Stanza Number: see under the S.no.			
S. no.	Myanmar	transliteration	English
28	နတ်ကြီးသူရဿတီ	Nat jee thura-thaddy	Great goddess is Saraswatī
29	ပင့်ချီခေါ်ချ	Pinn che khaw cha	Invite her and converse with her
30	စကားရလျက်	Sa gaah ya layet	Learn the words from her

44. These stanzas are popular for the simple poetic beauty of ending the poem.

Popular stanzas from Verse 55; Stanza Number: see under the S.no.			
S. no.	Myanmar	transliteration	English
12	သံချိုလင်္ကာ	Thaan cho lingah	In these sweet and poetic verses,
13	ထုံးပမာဖြင့်	Htone pamah fient	Setting the examples, illustrating with parables
14	နည်းနာတွေပြား	Nee nah htwey p-yar	Varieties of theories and techniques
15	မှတ်စိမ့်ကြားသည်	Hmat saint kjah thi	I tell you to learn
16	တခြား တတိယပိုင်းတည်း॥ ॥	Ta-char ta ti ya pine dee	Thus, I end the Third Part.

3.
Myanmar scripts

As mentioned in the beginning, the main objective of this book is "to present the international community with a piece of Myanmar classic cultural philosophy which has a significant political bearing." At the same time, the original source is also a classic Myanmar literature. Therefore, it is appropriate to include a brief account of the Myanmar alphabets. On the other hand, I am not a linguist nor a phonetician. Therefore, the reader is advised to consult the specialists in the subject of grammar, language and phonetics. My presentation here will serve as the starting point in exploring the Myanmar scripts and numbers.

The following internet sources were consulted in making the presentation. The URLs are accessed in October and September 2015.

1. http://www.omniglot.com/writing/sanskrit.htm
2. http://www.omniglot.com/writing/pali.htm
3. http://www.omniglot.com/writing/burmese.htm
4. https://en.wikipedia.org/wiki/Devanagari
5. http://spokensanskrit.de/
6. http://dictionary.tamilcube.com/pali-dictionary.aspx
7. http://www.eduplace.com/math/mthexp/g3/challenge/pdf/cm_g3_4_13.pdf
8. http://www.differencebetween.net/miscellaneous/culture-miscellaneous/difference-between-sanskrit-and-pali/
9. http://www.visiblemantra.org/pronunciation.html
10. http://thisbugslife.com/2012/10/15/international-phonetic-alphabets/
11. http://www.learning-hindi.com/
12. http://www.loc.gov/catdir/cpso/romanization/pali.pdf
13. https://archive.org/details/burmeseselftaugh00stjorich. This internet site is the source of *Burmese self-taught (in Burmese and Roman characters) with phonetic pronunciation.* (Thimm's system) by Richard Fleming St. Andrew St. John (1839-1919), published in 1911. St. John was a British orientalist. *I have followed St. John's teaching as the standard reference in my*

transliteration. Nevertheless, I have made the pronunciation simpler with the help of the text-to-speech software, mentioned earlier on the page 69.

Alphabets

The Myanmar alphabets are derived from the Indic Brāhmī script via the southern Brahmi Pallava script. Thus, it shares the common alphabetical ancestor with other Southeast Asian languages like Laos, Cambodia, and Thai. The Table-1 gives a simple version of the Myanmar alphabets. The Table-2 includes the Devanagari scripts with the phonetics. The Devanagari scripts are used in various languages all over India.

Table-1. Myanmar alphabets simplified				
M	က	ခ	ဂ	ဃ	င
R	ka	kha	ga	gha	ṅa
M	စ	ဆ	ဇ	ဈ	ည
R	ca	cha	ja	jha	ña
M	ဋ	ဌ	ဍ	ဎ	ဏ
R	ṭa	ṭha	ḍa	ḍha	ṇa
M	တ	ထ	ဒ	ဓ	န
R	ta	tha	da	dha	na
M	ပ	ဖ	ဗ	ဘ	မ
R	pa	pha	ba	bha	ma
M	ယ	ရ	လ	ဝ	သ
R	ya	ra	la	wa	tha
M	ဟ	ဠ	အ		
R	ha	La gyi	A		

| M = Myanmar |
| R = Romanized |

Table-2. Devanagari and Myanmar alphabets

Guttural	M	က	ခ	ဂ	ဃ	င
	D	क	ख	ग	घ	ङ
	IAST & IPA	ka /k/	kha /kʰ/	ga /g/	gha /gʱ/	ṅa /ŋ/
Palatal	M	စ	ဆ	ဇ	ဈ	ဉ
	D	च	छ	ज	झ	ञ
	IAST & IPA	ca /c, tʃ/	cha /cʰ, tʃʰ/	ja /ɟ, dʒ/	jha /ɟʱ, dʒʱ/	ña /ɲ/
Retroflex	M	ဋ	ဌ	ဍ	ဎ	ဏ
	D	ट	ठ	ड	ढ	ण
	IAST & IPA	ṭa /ʈ/	ṭha /ʈʰ/	ḍa /ɖ/	ḍha /ɖʱ/	ṇa /ɳ/
Dental	M	တ	ထ	ဒ	ဓ	န
	D	त	थ	द	ध	न
	IAST & IPA	ta /t̪/	tha /t̪ʰ/	da /d̪/	dha /d̪ʱ/	na /n/
Labial	M	ပ	ဖ	ဗ	ဘ	မ
	D	प	फ	ब	भ	म
	IAST & IPA	pa /p/	pha /pʰ/	ba /b/	bha /bʱ/	ma /m/
	M	ယ	ရ	လ	၀	သ
	D	य	र	ल	व	स
	IAST & IPA	ya /j/	ra /r/	la /l/	va /w, ʋ/	Sa /s/
Without group	M	သ (tha gyi)		ဟ	ဠ	အ
	D	श	ष	ह		
	IAST & IPA	śa /ɕ, ʃ/	Ṣa /ʂ/	ha /ɦ/	La [l̥a dźí]	A [ʔa]

M = Myanmar; D = Devanagari

IAST = International Alphabet of Sanskrit Transliteration

IPA = International Phonetic Alphabet

Translated and explained by Shwe Lu Maung

In the Myanmar alphabets, the three sibilant Sanskrit consonants श (śa), ष (ṣa) and स (sa) are not distinguished or discriminated. These words are represented by သ (tha), which is स (sa). In Hindi and Bengali स (sa) is pronounced just like the English alphabet 's' as in 'seat' or 'sing'.

Myanmar script is simplified in the sense that each alphabet is designed from the common base character of "o" that is "wa" in pronunciation and also is the 29th Myanmar alphabet. When we go to school we are placed in the class popularly called "wa tan" or "wa class." It is a *kindergarten*, before the Class or Grade 1. As a child, along with my classmates, I spend a good amount time writing o, o, o, o, (say wa, wa, wa, wa) and nothing but 'o' (wa) for days. There were no ruled notebooks in my days, but the slate boards (8x10 inches or ~20x25 cm writing size) are the mainstays. The slate pencils are used to write. With the homemade bamboo rulers, the kids have to draw ruled rows having about 2 mm in height and write many 'o's round and nice. It must be truly round. When the teacher is satisfied with our 'o's, the alphabets are taught, first reciting and then writing and reciting. This was in my days all over the country some 65 years ago. The books with the ruled lines are now in use in the affluent cities, but the slate board and pencil are still in place in the rural and low-income areas.

A slate board and pencil on sale at ebay.co.uk as of September, 2015

Each consonant of the Myanmar alphabets also constitutes a word having one or more meanings. New words are made by adding one or more auxiliary characters (diacritics) to the alphabets. The auxiliary characters, alone or combined up three, also represent the vowels, thus creating new sounds and words. A table of the auxiliary characters is given in the Table-3 and the examples of the consonants plus the auxiliary characters (diacritics) are given in the Table-4.

Table-3 vowels		
Myanmar	Devanagari	Romanized
အ	अ	a
အာ	आ	ā
ဣ also အိ	इ	i
အီ also ဤ	ई	ī
ဥ also အု	उ	u
အူ also ဦ	ऊ	ū
အေ also ဧ	ए	e
အဲ also အေး	ऐ	ai
အော also ဩ	ओ	o
အော် also ဪ	औ	au
အံ	अं	am
အား	अ:	āh

	Auxiliary characters (diacritics)	alphabet	word	Romanized
		က	က	k
1	ာ	က	ကာ	kā
2	ိ	က	ကိ	ki
3	ီ	က	ကီ	kī
4	ီ + း	က	ကီး	ki:
5	ု	က	ကု	ku
6	ူ	က	ကူ	kū
7	ူ + း	က	ကူး	kü
8	ံ	က	ကံ	kan
9	ာ + း	က	ကား	Kaar or kà
10	ေ	က	ကေ	kay
11	ေ + ့	က	ကေ့	ké
12	ေ + း	က	ကေး	kae
13	ဲ	က	ကဲ	kè
14	ဲ + း	က	ကဲး	kaè
15	ဲ + ့	က	ကဲ့	kaé
16	ေ + ာ	က	ကော	kau

Table-4. Construction of words with diacritics

Translated and explained by Shwe Lu Maung

Table-4. Construction of words with diacritics, continued				
	Auxiliary characters (diacritics)	alphabet	word	Romanized
17	၆ + ၁ +ိ	က	ကော်	kuaw
18	▢ or ▢	က	ကြ or ြ	kja or p-ya
19	ျ	က	ကျ	kja
20	၆ + ျ + ၁ +ိ	က	ကျော်	kjaw
21	္	မ	မှ	hma
22	္	မ	မှု	hmu
23	္ + း	မ	မှုး	hmü

In addition, there are five special words that are used in the sentences. These are given in Table-5

Table-5. Five special words		
	Special word	Pronunciation
1	၏	i [í]
2	၍	ī [i]
3	၌	hnight
4	၎	ywayt
5	သ	tha jee (big tha)

The use and meaning of the special words are given and explained below.

1. The word "၏" [í], pronounced ĕĕ

(1) The word "၏" [í] is used as auxiliary verb indicating

the end of an action as well as the completion of a sentence.

Example 1: သူထမင်းစား�__၏__ ။
Romanization: Thu htamin sa **ĕĕ**

English translation: He eats rice.
သူ (he) ထမင်း (rice) စား (eat) ၏ ။

Example 2:
အခေါင်တိုင်၏ ။ (part 2, Verse 40, Stanza 23)
Romanization: a khaun tine **ĕĕ**

English translation: Most magnificent above all.

(2) The word " ၏ " [í]   also carries the meaning and usage of the English word "of."

Example 1: သူ၏ အိမ်သည်ကားအေးချမ်းပါ၏ ။
Romanization: Thu **ĕĕ** in thi gah aye chan pa **ĕĕ**

English translation: His house is peaceful.

Example 2:
ပျား၏ နည်းထုံး၊ (Part 1, Verse 18, Stanza 7)
Romanization: piar **ĕĕ** knee htoone

English translation: the way of the bees,

In the above sentences, the word " ၏ " [í] indicates the possession.

2. The word "ဤ" [i] , pronounced ee
The word "ဤ" [i] means "this."

Example 1: ဤအိမ်သည်ကားအေးချမ်းပါ၏ ။
Romanization: **ee** in thi gah aye chan pa **ĕĕ**

English translation: This house is peaceful.
Example 2:
ဤသို့ရေသာ း (Part 2, Verse 23, Stanza 21)

Romanization:
ee thŏ yey thaar

English translation: Like this, it is counted.
Or, thus counted. ဤသို့ (**ee** thŏ) is "thus."

3. The word "၌", pronounced *hnight*

The word "၌" means in, at or on.

Example 1:
ကောင်းကျိုး ကိုယ်၌ တည်စေမင်း॥ ॥
(Part 1, Verse 2, Stanza 13)

Romanization:
kaung kjo ko hnight tae sae min

English translation: Institute in you good.

Example 2:
လမ်းမကြီး၌၊
(Part 1, Verse 20, Stanza 2)

Romanization:
Lan ma jee hnight

English translation: on the highway,

4. The word "၍" (ywayt)

The word "၍" (ywayt) means and or with, depending
on the context.

Example 1:
အမြဲရွက်၍
(Part 1, Verse 1, Stanza 12)

Romanization:
a mye ywat ywayt

English translation: carry always, and
Here, "ၡ" (ywayt) means "and."

Example 2:
ဆု(ကြီး)ရည်ၡ (Part 1, Verse 7, Stanza 12)

Romanization:
hsu jee yee ywayt

English translation: with the goal of Great Trophy
Here, "ၡ" (ywayt) means "with."

5. The word "သ" (tha jee or big tha)

The word "သ" (tha jee) is the Myanmar version of the
Devanagari ष (Ṣa /ṣ/) or स (Sa /s/), see the Table-2.
Devanagari and Myanmar alphabets. For example, the Sanskrit
मानुष (mAnuSa) or the Pali मनुस्स (manussa) is written မနုသ
(manutha) in Myanmar.

Punctuations

The punctuation marks in the Myanmar symbols are (1) 'ı'
called *par da* used as a comma, colon or semicolon and (2) 'ıı'
called *poat ma* used as the period or full stop at the end of a
sentence. In *Laukathara,* the stanzas are separated by the *par
da* 'ı', and the end of a set of the stanzas is marked with the *poat
ma* 'ıı'. The *poat ma* is made up of double *par da*. The double
poat ma (ıı   ıı) is known as the *poat ma jee* (big *poat ma*) and it
is used at the end of a verse or a paragraph.

Myanmar Grammar

The Myanmar grammar and writing system are the same
as those of the Indic languages.

Myanmar numerals

The Myanmar numeral system is the same as the modern common numeral system. The Myanmar numerals are given in the Table-6. It has the origin in the Indic numeral systems that came to Myanmar along with the Vedic literature, astrology and astronomy. As a matter of curiosity and comparison, the ancient Brahmi numerals are also included. It is believed by the scholars that the Indic and later Indo-Arabic numeral systems are derived from the ancient Brahmi numeral system. The Brahmi system, like in the Latin, has no zero. It has separate symbols for ten, twenty, thirty, hundred, and one thousand *et cetera*.

Table-6. Myanmar Numerals				
Modern common numerals		Myanmar numerals		Ancient Brahmi numerals
zero	0	၀	Thumya, thuñya	╳
one	1	၁	tit	▬
two	2	၂	nit	＝
three	3	၃	thon	≡
four	4	၄	lay	╀
five	5	၅	ngah	∩
six	6	၆	chaught	ᕼ
seven	7	၇	kanit	੧
eight	8	၈	sheat	↳
nine	9	၉	koo	૪
ten	10	၁၀	tisay	ᴂ

Appendices

Appendix-1: The Four Dhamma
ဓမ္မလေးမည်
Cross reference: Footnote 1, p 3
Part 1: Verse 4: Stanza 4.

The Four Dhamma are also known as the Four Noble Truths. These are:
1. Dukkha Sacca: The Noble Truth of Suffering.
2. Samudaya Sacca: The Noble Truth of the Cause (of Suffering)
3. Nirhodha Sacca: The Noble Truth of the Cessation (of Suffering);
4. Magga Sacca: The Noble Truth of the Path (leading to the Cessation of Suffering).

The Four Noble Truths are the First Sermon of Siddhārtha Gautama Buddha.[1] The First Sermon is known as the *Dhammacakkappavattana Sutta* (Pali) or *Dharmacakra Pravartana Sūtra* (Sanskrit), or the Setting in Motion of the Wheel of Law (English), delivered to his five disciples at the Deer Park, Sarnath, Varanasi, India, 2604 years ago, as per Burmese chronicles. Today, the Deer Park, Sarnath, Varanasi, India, is a major sacred pilgrim site. The First Sermon of Buddha can be read online at many Buddhist web pages. The "Cessation of Suffering" is Nirvana (Sanskrit) or Nibban (Pali). Thus, the Four Noble Truth is the path to Nirvana. Buddha attained the Enlightenment (Nirvana) at the age of 35, after 6 years of struggle. The day of First Sermon is also known as Dhamma-Cakra Day or Dhamma Day. It is celebrated by the Buddhists all over the world. In the 2015 Burmese calendar[2] it is on the full moon day of Second Waso month. In the Gregorian calendar it falls on the 31st of July 2015.

Buddha's date of birth and Parinibbana (passing away into Nibban) is still in dispute. According to a western school of scholars Buddha lived from 563-483 BCE.[3] According to the Burmese chronicles,

---

[1] Siddhārtha Gautama Buddha (624-544 BCE), as per Burmese records, https://en.wikipedia.org/wiki/Buddhist_calendar. Also see http://en.wikipedia.org/wiki/Gautama_Buddha

[2] http://www.burmeseclassic.com/calendar.php, accessed on July 11, 2015.

[3] See Clarence H. Hamilton. *Buddhism, a religion of infinite compassion*, The Liberal Arts Press, Inc., 1952, p xv.

Siddhārtha Gautama was born in 624 BCE. He went forth at age of 29, 595 BCE. After six years of ascetic life and meditation, attained Enlightenment at the age of 35, 589 BCE. Therefore, Buddha gave the First Sermon in the year 589 BCE, or 2604 years ago counting back from 2015.   The Burmese tradition recorded that Buddha taught Dharmacakra to the Five Ascetics on Saturday, full moon day of Waso. He entered Parinibbana on 13 May 544 BCE (Tuesday, Full Moon of Kason]. Burmese observed the 2500th year of Buddha Parinibbana in 1956. Buddhist calendar began on the day of Buddha Parinibbana.

The Burmese tradition teaches the children as follows.[4]

ဘုရားဖြစ်ခါ၊ မိဂဒါသို့၊ စကြာရွှေဖွား၊ ဖြန့်ချီသွားရှိ၊
ငါးပါးဝဂ္ဂီ၊ စုံအညီနှင့်၊ မဟီတသောင်း၊ တိုက်အပေါင်းမှ၊
ခဆောင်းကပ်လာ၊ နတ်ဗြဟ္မာအား၊ ဝါဆိုလပြည့်၊ စနေနေ့ဝယ်၊
ကြွေကြွေလျှံတက်၊ ဓမ္မစက်ကို၊ မိန့်မြွက်ထွေပြား၊
ဟောပြောကြားသည်။   ။
တရားနတ်စည်ရှုမ်းတယ်ကို။

It translates as follows.

"Upon the attainment of Enlightenment, Buddha went to Migata (Deer Park) where the Five Ascetics lived. From 10,000 worlds, the heavenly people Brahmans and Nats also gathered there. To them, Buddha delivered and explained the Wheel of Dhamma on Waso Full Moon Saturday. The heavenly drums of Dhamma were heard."

Appendix-2: The Three Doctrines of Buddha.
အနိစ္စနှင့်၊ ဒုက္ခအနတ္တား၊ သုံးပါးလက္ခဏာ

Cross reference: Footnote 8, p 8
Part 1; Verse 10; Stanza 1, 2, 3.

Anicca (အနိစ္စ) (Impermanency), Dukkha (ဒုက္ခ) (Suffering), and

---

[4] Dhammacakra Day, from the *Teachings to the Children, the jewels of the country*, (ရင်နှစ်သည်းချာ နိုင်ငံ့ရတနာ ဆုံးမစာများ) Department of Basic Education, Ministry of Education, Myanmar, 1992, page 39, in Burmese.

Anatta (အနတ္တ) (Not-self) are the three main doctrines of the Buddha's teachings. See *Antta Lakkhana Sutta, Samyutta Nikaya,* 22.59 (SN 22:59). It is a common practice to train the young Novices in meditation reflecting Anicca, Dukkha, Anatta.

An example, a piece of conversation between Buddha and his disciples, Bhikkhus, is given below.

"Bhikkhus, how do you conceive it: is form (Rupa) permanent or impermanent?" — "Impermanent, venerable Sir." — "Now is what is impermanent painful or pleasant?" — "Painful, venerable Sir." — "Now is what is impermanent, what is painful since subject to change, fit to be regarded thus: 'This is mine, this is I, this is my self'"? — "No, venerable sir."
(Source: http://www.accesstoinsight.org/tipitaka/sn/sn22/sn22.059.nymo.html, as of February 02, 2015).

Appendix-3: Five Aggregates of Mind and Body.
ပဉ္စခန္ဓာ
Cross reference: Footnote 9, p 8
P = Part 1; V = Verse 10; S = Stanza 8.

1. Matter Aggregate,
   (rūpa khandha) (ရုပ ခန္ဓာ)
2. Consciousness Aggregate,
   (viññāna khandha) (ဝိညာဏ ခန္ဓာ)
3. Feeling Aggregate,
   (vedanā) (ဝေဒနာ ခန္ဓာ)
4. Perception Aggregate,
   (saññā) (သညာဏ ခန္ဓာ)
5. Mental Formations Aggregate, (sankhāra khandha) (သခႤါရ ခန္ဓာ), composed of the remaining 50 mental concomitants or factors.

Source:
http://www.palikanon.com/english/intro-abhidhamma/chapter_iii.htm, as of February 02,2015.
Also see *Khandha Sutta: Aggregates,* in *Samyutta Nikaya,* 22.48

(SN 22:48) at:
http://www.accesstoinsight.org/tipitaka/sn/sn22/sn22.
048.than.html

Appendix-4: ကျောင်းတော်ခရီး
On the journey to the Temple
Cross reference: Footnote 16, p 16
P = Part 1; V = Verse 20; S = Stanza 1.

ကျောင်းတော်ခရီး (on the journey to the Temple):
The variant form is   ခြောင်းတော်ခရီး (on the path of the
journey).

ကျောင်း (kyauk) means school, temple, or herding, depending in
the context and use.

ခြောင်း   (krauk) means path, line, or passage, depending in the
context and use.

I was taught that it is ကျောင်းတော်ခရီး (on the journey to the
Temple), but not ခြောင်းတော်ခရီး (on the path of the journey).
The Temple is Maha Mrat Muni Temple of Rakhaing
Dhannyawaddy Kingdom. In the ancient Rakhaing Kingdom,
every road led to the Temple. I grew up in the City of Minbya
(City of King's Mangrove). It was a *prataw* mangrove, where
Nipa fruticans grows, not a *kine-taw* where *Rhizophora
mucronata* grows, before 1826 when the British established the
City of Minbya. In front of our house was the Min-Lan (The
King's Road) that led to the Maha Mrat Muni Temple, or simply
the Temple. From Minbya to Maha Mrat Muni is about 70 km
(~43 miles). From Mrauk-U to Maha Mrat Muni is about 36 km
(~ 22 miles), see the Google Earth direction map given below. In
Laukathara, Rakhine Thu Mrat is referring to the Min-Lan (The
King's Road) to the Temple. This is my learning from my parents
at home and teachers at school in my childhood, as per Rakhaing
tradition.

From Minbya to Maha Mrat Muni
via Mrauk-U
Google Earth direction, as of June 22, 2015

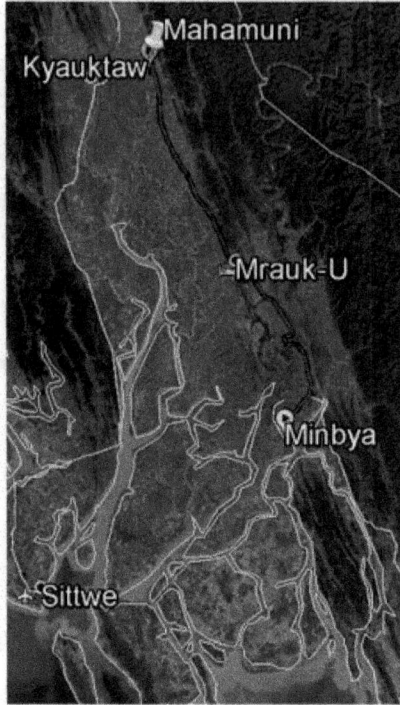

Sayagyi Min Thuu Wun used ကြောင်းတော်ခရီး၊ (on the path of the journey). He considered that ကျောင်း (kyauk) is the Bama (Burman) corruption of the Rakhaing word ကြောင်း (krauk) because the Bama people do not have the 'r' sound. For example, Rangoon is pronounced Yangon and ကြောင်း (krauk) is pronounced ကျောင်း (kyauk).

In this book, I have used ကျောင်းတော်ခရီး (on the journey to the Temple) as per Rakhaing tradition. Laukathara was written by Rakhine Thu Mrat in the days of King Min Hti (r.1279-1385 CE),[5]

---

[5] Also see Shwe Lu Maung. *Is Suu Kyi a racist?* Shahnawaz Khan Publication, USA, 2014, Appendix-1, Min Hti accountability, pp 121-123.

Laung Krut Dynasty (1237-1404 CE).[6] Laung Krut (also spelled Laung Kret) is in the ancient Kyein Province, which is now the Minbya Township of Myanmar Rakhine State. I learned from my maternal grandmother, Daw Hnin Pru (1871-1970), that in her young days large number of people in groups from Kyein Province went on foot or on boat to Maha Mrat Muni Festival, in the month of Tabaung (February-March). Even today, the festival lasts 2 weeks, traditionally centering the full moon day of Tabaung. The festival also hosts the Rakhaing boat race and wrestling. The festival became weak in the independent Burma due to the armed conflicts and poverty.

Appendix-5: Ten codes of King's conduct.
ဆယ်ထွေစောင့်ကြပ်၊ တရားကွပ်၍၊
Cross reference: Footnote 19, p 20
Part 1; Verse 23; Stanza 22, 23.

Ten codes of king's conduct in Pali, with Burmese within the parenthesis, are given below. In addition to the explanation by Min Thuu Wan, the Pali to English translations are consulted with the English-Pali dictionary at the: http://dictionary.tamilcube.com/pali-dictionary.aspx. It is also consulted with the Sri Lankan version of *Dasa Raja Dharma* from the book *Buddhist Ideals of Government* by Gunaseela Vitanage at http://www.filosofiaesoterica.com/ler.php? id=1727#.VMfdxU1owkI, last accessed on January 27, 2015.

1. Charity; Pali: dāna (ဒါန), meaning gift, charity, alms, alms-giving.
2. Self-sacrifice for the benefit of others; Pali: pariccāgo (ပရိစ္စာဂ), meaning abandonment, renunciation, sacrifice, expenditure, liberality.
3. Honesty and sincerity; Pali: ajjava (အဇ္ဇဝ), meaning honesty.
4. Humbleness; Pali: maddava (မဒ္ဒဝ), meaning softness, mildness, a soft thing, mild, gentle, soft.
5. Morality; Pali: sīla (သီလ), meaning nature, habit, moral practice, code of morality.

---

[6] Also see Shwe Lu Maung. *Burma Nationalism and Ideology*, University Press Ltd., Dhaka, 1989, p 8, Laung Kret Era.

6. Absence of hatred or practice of non-hatred; Pali: Akkodha (အကျ္ဘာ), meaning absence of hatred or anger.

Akkodha is the negative form of *Kodha*, which means hatred or anger.

7. Tolerance; Pali: Khanti (ခန္တိ), meaning tolerance.

8. Austerity; Pali: Tapa or Tapo (တပ), meaning self-mortification, penance, religious austerity.

9. Avoid torture; Pali: avihiṃsā (အဝိဟႎ သ), meaning humanity, absence of cruelty, Mercy.

10. Respect the public opinion; Pali: avirodha, (avirodhata, avirodhana) (အဝိ‌ရောဓန) meaning accordance, coherence, concord, friendliness, harmony, absence of opposition.

Appendix-6: The four friendship rules
                     or Four *saṅgaha-vatthūni*
                     သင်္ဂြိဟ်မှုလည်း၊ လေးခုအစု၊

Cross reference: Footnote 20, p 20
Part 2; Verse 23; Stanza 25, 26.

The four friendship rules are (1) *dāna*: charity or generosity, (2) *peyyavajja*: talking in kind, civilized and true words, (3) *atthacariyā*: wise or beneficial conduct, good action, e.g. welcoming, hospitality, looking after during sickness and giving a respectful burial at death; and (4) *samānattatā*: impartiality, equal treatment to all.

Burmese word သင်္ဂြိဟ် is from သင်္ဂဟ, Pali: Saṅgaha (सङ्गह)

The Burmese use of သင်္ဂြိဟ် has three meanings and uses depending on the context. It may mean (1) action, (2) treatment, and (3) undertaking funeral.

Appendix-7: "Pauk and Kyey"
ပေါက်နှင့်ကျေး
Cross reference: Footnote 22, p 23
Part 2; Verse 26; Stanza 2.

Pauk (ပေါက်) is the coral flower, *Erythrina variegata* or a similar species of flowering plant.

Kyey (ကျေး) is a parrot that has green wings and body, but with a bright red rosy beak. It may be a red-breasted parakeet (*Psittacula alexandri*), long-tailed parakeet (*Psittacula longicauda*), or vernal hanging parrot (*Loriculus vernalis*).

The shape and color of the beaks of these parrots are almost indistinguishable from the color and shape of the coral flower. The green color of the wing feathers and body plumage, and the red breast and beak effectively hide them among the green leaves and red flowers of the coral flower tree. The birds feed on the fruits and also serve as the pollinator.

Appendix-8: ဂြိုဟ် (ग्रह (grahaH) planet)
ဂြိုဟ်စာလည်းပေး (Offering to the planetary spirits)

Cross reference: Footnote 28, 103; p 25, 58
Part 2; Verse 28; Stanza 4, 13.

ဂြိုဟ် (GrahaH or Planets)			
Burmese (B)	Sanskrit (S)	Transliteration (S to E)	English (E)
တနင်္ဂနွေ	रवि	Ravi	Sun
တနင်္လာ	चान्द्र	Chandra	Moon
အင်္ဂါ	कुज	Kuja	Mars

ပုဒ္ဓဟူး	बुध	Budha	Mercury
ကြာသပတေး	सुरपतिगुरु	guru (Surapati-guru)	Jupiter
သောကြာ	शुक्र	Sukra (zukra)	Venus
စနေ	शनि	Sani (zani)	Saturn
ရာဟု	राहु	Rahu	Dragon's Head
ကိတ်	केतु	Ketu	Dragon's Tail

The Burmese word ဂြိုဟ် is the transliteration of Sanskrit ग्रह (grahaH) for planet. Burmese still follows the Vedic astrology and there are nine planetary spirits or Navagraha (Sanskrit: नवग्रह). A table of the Vedic astrological planets is given above. Up to date, it is a customary practice of the Burmese Buddhists to give food to the planetary spirits to earn their love, support, and blessing to ensure a success in every action and endeavor. The Burmese Buddhists believe that the alignment of the planets has great impact on human life as well as on the climate and agriculture; the phenomenon of the planetary alignment or movement can be controlled by nobody, but its effects are controlled by the planetary spirits. Therefore, it is vital to earn the favor of the spirits.

Notes.
The translations and transliteration of the Burmese and Sanskrit words are given here with the consultation at:
http://spokensanskrit.de.
and http://www.findyourfate.com/indianastro/grahas.htm.
Last visit to the websites was on July 14, 2015.

Appendix-9: *Thandae Puja* (သ‌‌ရွှေး‌ပူ‌ဇော်)

Cross reference: Footnote 29, 103; p 26, 58
Part 2; Verse 28; Stanza 14.

In the common Burmese belief and tradition, Thandae, "သ‌ရွှေး", is a ritual washing (shampooing) of the hair or head with fragrance and perfumes. This is also the understanding of Mun Thuu Wun in his book, e.g. page 169 for "သ‌ရွှေး" and "ဦး‌ခေါင်း သ‌ရွှေး". According to Mun Thuu Wun "သ‌ရွှေး" is Burmese version of Sanskrit "ဂ‌န္ဓိ" (pronounced *gandi*), (Sanskrit गन्ध, gandha: perfume).

Appendix-10: ကာ‌မ‌ဒေ‌ဝ (Kāma Deva)
   and လော‌က‌နတ် (Loka Nātha)
Cross reference: Footnote 32, p 28
Part 2; Verse 31; Stanza 1, 5.

The explanation given here is based on Min Thuu Wun's explanation in his book on the pages 142 and 162. Pali words in Devanagri scripts and meanings are added for better understanding of the terms.

Kāma is Pali (काम) for pleasure; lust; enjoyment; an object of sexual enjoyment.

There are four kinds of deva or Nātha (Pali). In Burmese, it is written and pronounced 'dewa' or 'nāt', respectively.

1. Kāma Deva (ကာ‌မ‌ဒေ‌ဝ) or Kāma-vasara (ကာ‌မာ‌ဝ‌စ‌ရ) Nātha are those who live in the 6 heavens of Buddhism plus the king of the human world. They are known as Kāma Deva because they are not free from Kāma. In other words, they are the sentient beings still filled with greed, anger, and delusion. Human king is known as Loka Nātha or sammuti nātha. According to the Tamil Pali dictionary sammuti (सम्मुति) means consent, authorization, permission; choice, selection; general consent or use. Nātha is a deva (also devadā, devatta).

2. Rupavacara Nātha or rupa loka Nātha, e.g. Rūpabrahma. Rupavacara means 'spheres of realms of forms'. Pali: रूपावचर; rūpāvacara; (rūpa + avacara): belonging to the world of form.

3. Arupavacara Nātha or arupa loka, e.g. Arūpabrahma. Pali: अरूपावचर, Arūpāvacara (arūpa + avacara): belonging to the world of formless; belonging to the realm of arūpins.

4. Visuddhi Nātha or visuddhideva. Pali: विसुद्धिदेव, visuddhideva: a holy person. Buddha.

Appendix-11: နန္ဒမူ (ရတနာမြဂူ၊ နန္ဒမူဠ်၊)
The jewel jade Cave of Nandamu
မဉ္ဇူပန်း Mitzu Flower

Cross reference: Footnote 39, p 33
Part 2; Verse 34; Stanza 26, 27.

It is believed that the jade Cave of Nandamu was in the Gandhamadana Ridge. Today, the internet hosts a number of articles on Gandhamadana of Hindu mythology. Mount Gandhamadana is also the highest peak and popular tourist site on the Indian Pamban Island in the Palk Strait between Indian Subcontinent and Sri Lanka. Some scholars believe that Gandhamadana was the name of a mountain ridge in the northern Himalaya. The Burmese story of the cave and flower goes as below.

According to the Buddhist legends, there is a mountain ridge known as Gandhamadana in the Himalaya Mountains. Nandamūlaka Valley is in the Gandhamadana mountain ridge. In the valley, there are three caves, known as (1) the golden cave (Suvanna-guha), (2) the jewel-ratana cave (Mani-guha), and (3) the silver cave (Rajata-guha). The jewel cave is called ratana-mya-gu (ရတနာမြဂူ) or the cave of jewel jade in Burmese literature. At the entrance of the jewel cave the celestial flower tree known as Manjusaka Deva (Mitzu in Burmese) grows.[7] In the jewel cave, the legendary Pacceka Buddha (pratyekabuddha, pratyekabodhisattva) named Matanga lived before the birth of Siddhārtha Gautama, who became Gautama Buddha. According to the legends,

[7] U Chit Tin (Sayagyi), The story of Pacceka Buddha Matanga, http://www.skepticfiles.org/mys3/matanga.htm, last accessed on February 9, 2015.

Manjusaka tree was one yojana high and one yojana wide. One yojana is defined to be about 8.0 km or 5 miles, as per Wikipedia article on "yojana." When Pacceka Buddha Matanga, in his ascetic life, first reached the cave the Manjusaka flowers burst into bloom all at once.[8] Pacceka Buddha is a Silent Buddha or Solitary Buddha because, although having gained enlightenment for themselves, they do not propagate the doctrines.[9] Manjusaka flower is identified with *Madhuca longifolia* of the Sapotaceae family.[10] Madhu in Pali means honey. It is known as Mahua in Bengal and its tender leaves are silky pinkish violet, very lovely and beautiful, and can be mistaken as the flowers. The flowers are greenish yellow, sweet like honey and edible. However, in China, Korea and Japan, Manjusaka or Man Jyu Sha Ge, is the name for cluster amaryllis (*Lycoris radiata*) and popular with a fascinating legend.

Appendix-12: Four kinds of lion လေးတွေအရှိုး၊ ခြင်္သေ့မျိုး
Cross reference: Footnote 50, p 38
Part 2; Verse 38; Stanza 9, 10;

Four kinds of lion, (လေးတွေအရှိုး၊ ခြင်္သေ့မျိုး) are explained by Min Thuu Wun, Laukathara Pyo, page 161.

1. တိဏသီဟ (तिण (Pali) tiṇa; grass; सीह (Pali): sīha; a lion); Brown lion that eats grass.

2. ကာဠသီဟ (काळ (Pali) kāḷo; Black; सीह (Pali): sīha; a lion); काळसीह: kāḷasīha. Black lion that eats grass.

3. ပဏ္ဍုသီဟ (पण्डरो (Pali) paṇḍaro; White, pale, yellowish; सीह (Pali): sīha; a lion). Pale lion that eats meat.

4. ကေသရသီဟ (केसरसीह (Pali) kesarasīha; a maned lion; Maned lion that eats meat.

The Pali words, transliterations, and meanings are from . http://dictionary.tamilcube.com/pali-dictionary.aspx.

---

[8] Reginald A. Ray, Buddhist Saints in India: A Study in Buddhist Values and Orientations, Oxford University Press, 1999, p 216.
[9] http://lara88v.blogspot.com/2010/05/manjusaka-celestial-flower.html, last accessed on February 9, 2015.
[10] Ibid, and https://www.flickr.com/photos/sajan164/6885090110/in/photostream/

Appendix-13: The Five Prowess (ဗလင်္ဂါးတန်)
Cross reference: Footnote 54, 56, 57; p 41
Part 2; Verse 40; Stanza 1, 3, 18.

1. ကာယ + ဗလ
Prowess of Body or Physical Prowess

(ကာယ): Pali: काय; kāya; the body.

(ဗလ): Pali: बल; bala; strength; power; force; an army; military force.

2. ဉာဏ + ဗလ
Prowess of Wisdom

(ဉာဏ): Pali: ज्ञान; ñāṇa; wisdom; insight.

3. ဘောဂ + ဗလ
Prowess of Wealth

(ဘောဂ): Pali: भोग; bhoga; possession; wealth; enjoyment; the coil of a snake.

4. မိတ္တ + ဗလ
Prowess of Friendship

(မိတ္တ): Pali: मेत्ती mettī; Friendship, good will, love, charity.

5. စာရိတ္တ + ဗလ
Prowess of Character

(စာရိတ္တ): Pali: चिरत; carita; character; behavior; life.

Appendix-14: Four Gati (ဂတိလေးပါး)
Cross reference: Footnote 69, 72; p 44, 45
Part 2; Verse 42; Stanza 11.

Rakhine Thu Mrat wrote Four Gati (ဂတိလေးပါး). Min Thuu Wun believes that it actually is Four Agati (အဂတိလေးပါး) or Four Wrong Paths, in his explanation under the 'gati' (ဂတိ), in his book Laukathara, page 126. He believes that 'a' (အ) was missed out in the spelling, in the interest of poetic regularity in rhyming, a common practice of the poets.

ဂတိ (gati) is Pali: गति; gati; going; career; course; passing on to another existence; destiny; behavior.

According to Min Thuu Wun the four 'agati' are:

(1) ဆန္ဒာဂတိ (ဆန္ဒာ + ဂတိ) from Pali: चिन्ता; cintā ; thinking ; thought ; consideration + गति; gati, as described above; meaning a course of life guided by the thoughts.

(2) ဒေါသဂတိ (ဒေါသ + ဂတိ) from Pali: दोस; dosa; anger; corrupting; defect; fault + गति; gati, as described above; meaning a course of life guided by anger.

(3) ဘယာဂတိ (ဘယာ + ဂတိ) from Pali: भय; bhaya; fear; fright + गति; gati, as described above; meaning a course of life guided by fear.

(4) မောဟာဂတိ (မောဟ + ဂတိ) from Pali: मोह; moha; stupidity; delusion + गति; gati, as described above; meaning a course of life guided by delusion.

Rakhine Thu Mrat original Burmese:
ဂတိလေးပါး၊ မမှားစေအောင်၊

Min Thuu Wun's interpretation:
အဂတိတရားလေးပါးကို မလိုက်စားမိရအောင် စောင့်ရှောက်ရှို၊
In English it can be translated as follows:
(A king) "must guide himself to stay away from the Four Agati (wrong) practices."

Appendix-15: Glossaries of Part 3, Verse 49, S = Stanza
Cross reference: Footnote 110, 111; p 59

S1. ဟောရဂန္ထ (Pali: होरा गन्थ, horā gantha): astrological book

S2. ဂဏန (Pali: गणना, gaṇanā): The number, counting or calculation. Today, the Myanmar word for arithmetic is "ganan thancha" (ဂဏန်း သင်္ချာ) which is "gaṇanā saṅkhyā" (गणना सङ्ख्या) in Pali.

S5. ပုဏ္ဏား Ponna is a Vedic priest.

S12. ဗြိဟာတ် From Varāhamihira, 505-587 CE, Indian astronomer, mathematician, and astrologer. Here it refers to his books.

S12. ရာဇမတ္တာတ် Min Thuu Wun describes it to be a kind of Vedic calculation text in his book, page 157. In Pali Raja (राजा, king) and mataM (मतं, injunctions) will mean the injunctions of the king. It probably is a Vedic branch of predicting the king's fate and affairs.

S13. ကိန်းဆန် Min Thuu Wun describes ကိန်းဆန် (Kimcan) a kind of Vedic calculation in his book page 120. It probably is the Burmese version of Pali Kimcana, which means "what if"? If so, it will be a discipline of Prazna (Sanskrit: प्रश्न) (also Prasna), which literally means 'inquiry' or astrological inquiry into the future, as per definition given at http://spokensanskrit.de (date of accession February 03, 2015).

S13. ဒူးဝန်း Min Thuu Wun describes ဒူးဝန်း (dhuvan) an astrological method in his book page 140. It probably is a Burmese word adopted from the Sanskrit धुवन, dhuvana, which means fire in Vedic as per definition at http://www.sanskritdictionary.com. It is something to do with the funeral burning ritual as per Atharva-veda.
See *Atharva-veda Samhita* Volume 8,

Edited by Charles Rockwell Lanman, publisher Motilal Banarsidass, Delhi, 1971, page 854.

S14. ဂြိုဟ်သွန်း from Pali: gahasañcāradīpaka, meaning ephemeris. The planetary position in the orbit or path.

S14. မန်းကပ် (Mann-Kap) calculation of the planetary alignment, eg. the alignment of the five planets, viz. Jupiter, Mars, Mercury, Venus, Saturn, as per explanation of Min Thuu Wun. I failed to find this word in Pali Devanagari script.

S16. အသိတိစုတ် (Athiti-sut), Burmese from Pali: असीति; asīti, meaning eighty. In the Rakhaing dialect, စုတ် (*sut*, from *Sutta*) means reciting, strictly used in reciting the magical words, mantras or religious verses, repeatedly to achieve a desired effect. Here, Athiti-sut may mean eighty recitals. However, Min Thuu Wun defined it a Vedic analytical method of Vedic elements (Pali: धातु, dhātu) in his interpretation, page 103.

S17. ဓာတ် (Pali: धातु, dhātu); the basic elements of the universe such as earth, heat, water, and air.

S20. သတ္တာဝီသ The twenty seven (lunar mansions, Nakshatras, in Vedic astrology), see the Table-1.

#	Name (Sanskrit)	Devanagari	Burmese
	Table-1. List of the 27 *Nakshatras*		
1	Ashwini	अश्विनि	အသွဝနီ
2	Bharani	भरणी	ဘရဏီ
3	Kritika	कृत्तिका	ကြတ္တိကာ
4	Rohini	रोहिणी	ရောဟိဏီ
5	Mrigashīrsha	मृगशीर्षा	မိဂသီ
6	Ārdrā	आर्द्रा	အဒြ

7	Punarvasu	पुनर्वसु	ပုန္ဗဝသု
8	Pushya	पुष्य	ဖုဿ
9	Āshleshā	आश्लेषा	အသလိဿာ
10	Maghā	मघा	မာဃ
11	Pūrva or Pūrva Phalgunī	पूर्व फाल्गुनी	ပြုဗ္ဗဖလဂုနီ
12	Uttara or Uttara Phalgunī	उत्तर फाल्गुनी	ဥတ္တရ ဖလဂုနီ
13	Hasta	हस्त	ဟသ္တ
14	Chitra	चित्रा	စိၾတ
15	Svātī	स्वाति	သြာတိ
16	Viśākhā	विशाखा	ဝိသာခါ
17	Anurādhā	अनुराधा	အနုရာဓ
18	Jyeshtha	ज्येष्ठा	ေဇ႒
19	Mula	मूल	မူလ
20	Pūrva Ashādhā	पूर्वाषाढ़ा	ပြုဗ္ဗသဠ္
21	Uttara Aṣāḍhā	उत्तराषाढ़ा	ဥတ္တရသဠ္
22	Śrāvaṇa	श्रावण	သရဝဏ္
23	Śrāviṣṭha or Dhanishta	श्रविष्ठा or धनिष्ठा	ဓနသိ႒
24	Shatabhisha or Śatataraka	शतभिषा or शततारका	သတဘိသ္သ
25	Pūrva Bhādrapadā	पूर्वभाद्रपदा	ပြုဗ္ဗဘၾဒပိုဒ္
26	Uttara Bhādrapadā	उत्तरभाद्रपदा	ဥတ္တရဘၾဒပိုဒ္
27	Revati	रेवती	ေရဝတီ

The table 1 is based on the information collected from
http://en.wikipedia.org/wiki/List_of_Nakshatras,
and https://en.wikipedia.org/wiki/Burmese_zodiac.
The Wiki articles were accessed in March and December 2015.

S22. မြင်းမိုရ် (MyinMor): Mt. Meru of Vedic Cosmology. All the planets, including the sun revolves around Mt. Meru. It is the center of the universe.

S21. လှည့်ထက်နက်သတ်   planets, *Nakshatras* of Vedic cosmology, see the Table-1.

S22. မြင်းမိုရ်ပတ်သား Revolve around the Mt. Meru

S23. ဒွါဒသရာသီ   (ဒွါဒသ (Pali: द्वादस, dvādasa: twelve)   + ရာသီ (Pali: राशि ; rāsi ; a sign of the zodiac). Twelve Zodiac Houses of Vedic astrology. See the Table-2.

Table 2. The Burmese Vedic Twelve Zodiac Houses			
#	Burmese	Sanskrit	English	Latin
1	မိသာ	मेष	*Meṣa*	Aries
2	ပြိသာ	वृषभ	*Vṛṣabha*	Taurus
3	မေထုန်	मिथुन	*Mithuna*	Gemini
4	ကရကဋ်	कर्क	*Kark*	Cancer
5	သိဟ်	सिंह	*Siṃha*	Leo
6	ကန်	कन्या	*Kanyā*	Virgo
7	တု	तुला	*Tulā*	Libra
8	ဗြိစ္ဆာ	वृश्चिक	*Vṛścika*	Scorpio
9	ဓနု	धनुष	*Dhanus*	Sagittarius
10	မကာရ	मकर	*Makara*	Capricorn
11	ကုံ	कुम्भ	*Kumbha*	Aquarius
12	မိန်	मीन	*Mīna*	Pisces

The Table-2 is based on the description of Min Thuu Wun in his book page 148, and Wikipedia article at: http://en.wikipedia.org/wiki/Hindu_astrologytwelve rasi

S29, S30. ဉပ္ပါတ်အာယု၊ စဉ်းမှုတတ်ပွန်၊

In simple interpretation of the above clauses, it means to having skill of calculating or predicting the danger of the eclipse that may have impact on life.

The literal meanings are given below.

ဥပ္ပါတ် Pali: उपद्व, upaddava: misfortune, distress, danger.

အာယုစဉ်း (အာယုစန္ဒ) (အာယုစန်းတွက်နည်း) Ayuchanda, as per Min Thuu Wun's explanation in his book, pages 103 and 173, is a kind of calculation of the good or bad effect of eclipses. As per definition of the Pali words it may have something to do with the determination of rhythms of life when an eclipse occurs. Please consult a Vedic astrologer if you have interest.

အာယု Plai: आयु, āyu: Life

စဉ်း (စန္ဒ) Pali: छन्द, chanda: metrics, prosody, impulse, will, wish.

S37. ကိတ္တိ Pali: कित्तिमन्तु, kittimantu: famous .

Appendix-16: Glossaries of Part 3, Verse 51, S = Stanza
Cross reference: Footnote 114, 115; p 62

S1. ဥဒည်း (uddin) from Pali: उदेति, udeti: To rise, of the sun.

S1. မဇ္ဈင် (mizjin) from Pali: मज्झण्ह, majjhaṇha: the noon, midday.

S3. သည်းသာ (sesa) from Pali: संझा, sañjhā: the evening.

S4. ဂါထာ (gatha) from Pali: गाथा, gāthā: verse or stanza (of the prayers or hymns in this case).

S6. ကာယ (kaya) from Pali: काय, kāya: a heap, a collection, the body.

S6. သိဒ္ဓိ (Thidhi) from Pali: सिद्धि (siddhi) Formation, accomplishment; success, prosperity. Also see footnote 52 at V39, p39.

S6. ကာယာသိဒ္ဓိ (Kayah Thidhi or kayā siddhi) "body perfection" can be achieved through meditation or Yoga. It is believed that with the achievement of *kaya siddhi* a person can levitate, make invisible, and travel through the air.

S7. တရိ (Tari) from Sanskrit: त्रि, tri: three

S7. သညာ (Thanyar) from Pali: सञ्ञा, saññā: sense, perception, mark, name, recognition, gesture.

S7. တရိသညာ (Tari Thanyar or Tri saññā) probably refers to the three different sets of mantras or prayers assigned for the three periods of the day, morning (sun rise), noon and evening (sun set), in the given context. Min Thu Wun also explained in this meaning. On the other hand, saññā or perception is a very big subject in Buddhism as well as in other schools of philosophy and science.

S10. ပရမိသွာ (Paramethaw, but read Parameshaw), a title of Lord Shiva, as per Min Thuu Wun, in his book, page 144.

Lord Shiva has 108 titles.[11] The Burmese version Paramethaw comes from the Sanskrit word परमेश्वर, paramezvaram, meaning Supreme Lord.[12] According to a Wikipedia article,[13] Parameshwara (God) is a combination of three words (parama + Ish + vara), that is (supreme + master + excellent) or Excellent Supreme Master.

S11. မဟာဝိနဲ့ (Mahavinnay), also known as မဟာဝိနာယက (Mahavinayaka) is Lord Ganesh or Ganesha (Sanskrit: गणेश, Gaṇeśa) of Hindu Pantheon, well known for having an elephant head on human body, and most popular. There are numerous online articles on Ganesh. The story behind his birth and elephant head is indeed most intriguing.[14]

---

[11] http://www.rudraksha-ratna.com/108-names-of-shiva_28.html5

[12] http://spokensanskrit.de/index.php?
tinput=paramezvara&script=&direction=SE&link=yes

[13] http://en.wikipedia.org/wiki/Parameshwara_(God)

[14] For example see
http://en.wikipedia.org/wiki/Mythological_anecdotes_of_Ganesha#Elephant_hea d.

S13. နတ်စန္ဒီ (natsandi or Goddess Sandi)

Chandi (Sanskrit: चण्डी, Caṇḍī) or Chandika or Ran-Chandi (Caṇḍīka) is the supreme Goddess of Devi Mahatmya (Sanskrit: Devīmāhātmyam, देवीमाहात्म्यम्) also known as Chamunda or Durga as mentioned in *Durga Saptashati,* as Wikipedia definition.[15]

Appendix-17: Glossaries of Part 3, Verse 52, **S**= Stanza
Cross reference: Footnote 116, 118; p 63, 64

S1

ဂြဟသန္တိ (ဂြဟ + သန္တိ): (Graha {Sanskrit: ग्रह} + Shanti {Sanskrit: शांति, shaantiH: peace}, Literally, it means "appeasing the planets or planetary gods".

It is explained by the hindupriestservices.com[16] as follows.

"Graha Shanti:
Graha Shanti pooja is done to appease the particular planet which is an adverse position in one's horoscope or to enhance the effect of a positive influence of a particular planet. Each planetary power has to be appeased in a different way and thus the pooja ritual."

S3

ဗလိပူဇော် (Bali puja or Bali worship)

Bali (Sanskrit: बलि), as per Sanskrit dictionary,[17] is the Emperor of demons. He was the grandson of Prahlada and son of the demon Virochana in the Hindu pantheon.[18] Literally, in both Sanskrit and Pali, 'bali' also means "an offering or propitiatory oblation".[19]

As per online article:[20]

---

[15] http://en.wikipedia.org/wiki/Chandi. There are namy online articles on Chandi.

[16] http://hindupriestservices.com/pooja4321/pooja.html

[17] http://dictionary.tamilcube.com/sanskrit-dictionary.aspx,

[18] http://btg.krishna.com/lord-vamana-resolves-universal-conflict

[19] http://spokensanskrit.de and http://dictionary.tamilcube.com/pali-dictionary.aspx.

[20] http://www.trambakeshwar.com/narayannagbali.htm

"Narayan Nag*bali* consists of two different rituals. Narayan *bali* is done to get rid of ancestral curse (Pitru dosh /Pitru Shaap) while Nag *bali* is done to get rid of sin performed by killing a snake, specially Cobra which is worshiped in India. It can be performed only at Trimbakeshwar."

Its significance is explained as follow.

"For Problems like Bhoot Pishach Badha (disturbances by the ghosts), unsuccessful in Business, Waste of Money, Family health Problems, Argument with others, Educational hindrances, Marriage Problems, Accidental Death, Unnecessary expenses, Health problems in many family members, All kind of Curse (shrap). . . . It gives good health, success in business and career and fulfills wishes. It is a three day ritual on a particular day and time (muhurta). On the first day, the devotees should take a holy bath in Kushavarta and resolve to give dashdaan (give ten things in charity). After offering prayers at the Trimbakeshwar temple, they go to the dharmashala at the confluence of rivers Godavari and Ahilya for performing Narayan Nagbali."

As per Min Thuu Wun's explanation in his book page 149, Bali is a puja to the Nāt or spirits. Prime Minister U Nu performed Bali puja or propitiatory offering of food to the Spirits at Mt. Popa, Central Burma in 1959, when he was pushed out of the office by General Ne Win in 1958. At that time, I was too young to understand what it was.

S4

ဂြိုဟ် (gro): Burmese version of Graha (Sanskrit: ग्रह) or planet.

S5

ဝေဒင် (vedin): Burmese version of Vedic.

S6

မန္တန် (mandan): a Burmese version of mantra.

S7

စက္က (sakka): a Burmese version of Sanskrit: चाक्र (cAkra), meaning circular.

S8

မဏ္ဍလ (mandala): Burmese version of Sanskrit: मण्डल (Maṇḍala), which is a spiritual and ritual symbol of the Universe in Hinduism and Buddhism. There are many online articles on Mandala. This is the source of the name of the City of Mandalay, supposed to be the center of universe.

S9

တစ်ရာ့ရှစ်ကွင်း Burmese for "108 geometric icons" that represents many things in Hinduism and Buddhism. A few relevant concepts are given below.[21]

Sri Yantra in Hinduism: On the Sri Yantra there are marmas where three lines intersect, and there are 54 such intersections. Each intersection has "masculine and feminine," plus "shiva and shakti" qualities. Therefore, 54 times 2 equals 108.
Thus, there are 108 points that define the Sri Yantra as well as the human body.

Sanskrit alphabet: There are 54 letters in the Sanskrit alphabet. Each has masculine and feminine, shiva and shakti. 54 times 2 is 108.

Astrology: There are 12 constellations, and 9 arc segments called namshas or chandrakalas. 9 times 12 equals 108. Chandra is the moon, and kalas are the divisions within a whole.

Planets and Houses: In astrology, there are 12 houses and 9 planets. 12 times 9 equals 108.

Buddhism: Some Buddhists carve 108 small Buddhas on a walnut for good luck. Some ring a bell 108 times to celebrate a new year. There are said to be 108 virtues to cultivate and 108 defilements to avoid.

In Burma, Buddha Foot Mandala is made up with 108 geometric designs and signs.

---

[21] The information are directly taken from http://www.swamij.com/108.htm. Please visit the web site for more information.

S10

အမ်း (Amm) or the sacred sign: In Burmese, အမ်း (Amm) means laying down a mandala with the recitation of mantras. It actually is the Burmese version of "**Om/Aum** (ॐ; in Devanagari as ओं *oṁ* [õː], औं *auṃ* [ə̃ĩ], or ओ३म् *om* [õːːm]) is a mantra and mystical sound of Hindu origin (geographically India and Nepal), sacred and important in various Dharmic religions such as Hinduism, Buddhism and Jainism. The syllable is also referred to as **omkara** (ओंकार *oṃkāra*) or **aumkara** (औंकार *auṃkāra*), literally "om syllable", and in Sanskrit it is sometimes referred to as *praṇava*, literally "that which is sounded out loudly"".[22]
Please note the similarity of the Burmese and Devanagari writings.

S11

ဝိတာန် (vitan): from Pali: वितान, vitāna: a canopy.

S19

ဥပဒ် (Upad) from Pali उपद्रव, upaddava: misfortune, distress, danger.

S 30 and 31

ပန်းငါးမည်ဖြင့်၊ ဆောက်တည်မပျက်၊
Wear the Five Flowers,
Perform steadfast and strong.

Here, "Wear Five Flowers" means to keep five precepts of religious conduct or sila, which are (1) not to kill, (2) not to steal, (3) not to get intoxicated (4) not to adulterate (or not to have sex in this context) (5) not to tell lie. These are the five basic precepts that everybody must keep at all time, in Buddhist culture.

---

[22] The explanation of Om is directly quoted from
http://en.wikipedia.org/wiki/Om. Please visit the web site for more information.

Appendix-18: Book 3 Verse 53 Stanza 32
Cross reference: Footnote 120, p 66

စနက္က (Zanakka):

Min Thuu Wun identified စနက္က (Zanakka) the advisor (Chief
Teacher Ponna) of Chandra Gupta (စန္ဒဂုတ်) and mentioned that
he is known in Sanskrit as Sanakya (စာဏက္ၚ) in his book, page 134.
If so, Zanakka (စနက္က) referred here must be Chanakya, the chief
advisor of Chandragupta Maurya (Sanskrit: चन्द्रगुप्त मौर्य;) (340 BC
– 298 BC), who was the founder of the Maurya Empire. Chanakya
is believed to be Kautilya or Vishnu Gupta, the author of the most
famous treatise called *Arthasastra* or Economics. There are many
credible articles on him and his book, available online. The brief
information given here is taken, on July 22, 2015, from:

1. https://en.wikipedia.org/wiki/Chanakya,
and
2. http://en.wikipedia.org/wiki/Chandragupta_Maurya

Index of words and subjects
(v= verse; p= page; fn= footnote)

For your information:
Books on Myanmar (Burma) by Shwe Lu Maung

1. Burma Nationalism and Ideology, University Press Ltd. (1989)
ISBN-13: 978-9840511143

2. The Price of Silence: Muslim-Buddhist war of Bangladesh and Myanmar,
Pbook ISBN-13: 978-1928840-03-9 (2005)
Ebook ISBN 13: 978-1928840-04-6 (2011)
Shahnawaz Khan Publications

3. The Rakhine State Violence:
Vol. 1: The Rakhaing Revolution (2014),
Pbook ISBN 13: 978-192880-09-1;
Ebook ISBN 13: 978-1-928840-12-1 (2014)
Shahnawaz Khan Publications

4. The Rakhine State Violence Vol. 2: The Rohingya (2014)
Pbook ISBN-13: 978-1928840107
Ebook ISBN 13: 978-1-928840-13-8
Shahnawaz Khan Publications

5. Is Suu Kyi a racist? (2014)
Pbook ISBN-13: 978-1928840114
Ebook ISBN 13: 978-1-928840-14-5
Shahnawaz Khan Publications

Tagore's poems published by Shahnawaz Khan

Rabindranath Tagore: Gitanjali (1922)
ISBN 13: 978-1928840-05-3
Shahnawaz Khan Publications, 2014

Rabindranath Tagore: The Gardener (1917)
ISBN 13: 978-1-928840-08-4
Shahnawaz Khan Publications, 2012

Notes

www.ingramcontent.com/pod-product-compliance
Lightning Source LLC
Chambersburg PA
CBHW070800290326

41931CB00011BA/2090